STOCK MARKETS AND FINANCIAL JOURNALISM

S.K. AGGARWAL

SHIPRA

DEDICATION

This book is dedicated to the loving memory of my father, Mr. M.M. Lal Aggarwal and my mother, Smt. Lila Wati, without whose blessings and inspiration, I would not have been able to undertake this work. This book is also dedicated to my wife, Kamal, my son, Aditya and daughter, Asmita.

ISBN : 81-7541-012-4

First Published in India in 1998

Published by :
SHIPRA PUBLICATIONS
115-A, Vikas Marg, Shakarpur,
Delhi-110092 (India)
Ph : 2458662, 2200954 Fax : 2458662
Email : shipra@writeme.com

Laser Typeset by :
Sunshine Graphics
Delhi-110032

Printed at :
Nice Printing Press,
Delhi

Preface

A few years ago, I was asked to deliver lectures on financial journalism at the Indian Institute of Mass Communication (IIMC) and other places. I went about in search of material, but found hardly any. It was then that I decided to write a comprehensive book on this subject.

In recent years, and especially in the wake of liberalisation of economy, there has been tremendous growth in the publication of financial magazines and newspapers. Even general papers have expanded to cover financial news. The electronic media has not lagged behind either. It has started giving special bulletins on stock markets and financial news.

This has opened new opportunities for journalists. An increasing number of journalists today are joining financial journalism for two reasons. One, for better emoluments. Two, for good job prospects. Most of them have attained both. I can say from my, experience that about a dozen of my students have changed newspapers thrice and each time they have improved their position. Some of them have become special correspondents in a short span of four years, drawing a salary of Rs. 15,000 to 20,000. Journalists at the desk have done equally well.

Not only young journalists are attracted to this profession, even CAs and MBAs are flocking to it. Some of them have joined multinationals after a short stint in *The Economics Times*, and are now drawing a salary of Rs. 40,000.

Today, this profession requires specialisation. Gone are the days, when a journalist could be called upon to perform multifarious jobs. This job requires special knowledge and training. Hence, I have tried to help the entrants to prepare themselves for the new challenges.

With the help of this book, I have attempted to give the reader an idea about the functioning of the various aspects of the stock and financial markets. The book covers not only the theoretical aspects but also the operational aspects of various subjects.

I have also tried to enlarge the scope of this book to help students of MBA and MBE who may be joining financial newspapers and magazines.

The stock market condition is the barometer of health of the economy of a country. It helps industries to mobilise huge funds without the liability of paying heavy interest on collections. Our stock market is suffering because it lacks honesty, efficiency and transparency. Our corporate sector by and large has not developed the culture of building confidence in the investors and giving them good returns. Today, the investors have diverted their funds to NBFCs which have garnered Rs. 20,000 crores and some of them have even refused more subscription.

It is also true that Sebi in its enthusiasm to streamline the market has over-regulated it, resulting in its strangulation. One such case is the abolition of *badla* system. Admittedly, *badla* was bad and led to payment crisis, but Sebi has not been able to provide any substitute for it.

The OTECI was set up to help medium size units to raise funds from the markets, but the exchange is plagued by lack of liquidity and depth. The financial institutions which were responsible for its birth have failed to promote it. The National Stock Exchange has brought transparency into its functioning and is doing exceedingly well, but it has not been able to broadbase itself and its large turnover is restricted to only a few scrips.

The Mutual Fund industry in India is really a late 80's phenomena. Prior to that, the scene was dominated by the Unit Trust of India, which even today, is the biggest player. All this changed dramatically when this sector was thrown open to private sector. The new private sector mutual funds got off to a rousing start in the 90s and collected Rs. 11,000 crores in the wake of the 1992 stock boom.

Unfortunately, the present situation is dismal. These Funds have not ensured a good return to investors. Most of them have not even given 18 per cent return which one gets from the corporate deposits. Secondly, their prices on the bourses are at substantial discounts to net asset value, indicating erosion in investor confidence.

It is an accepted fact, however, that the computerisation of stock exchanges has revolutionised its functioning and has brought about a transparency to a great extent. An effort is being made now to set up a bank to finance brokers and help stock exchanges to get over liquidity problems. The setting up of a central depository will reduce the delay and inefficiency in dealing with share transfers.

If we wish to register an economic growth rate of 10 to 12 per cent, which is being witnessed in some of the Asian countries, called Asian Tigers, we have to strengthen our stock markets. There is no other option. Sebi has made a lot of changes to tone up the market, but its impact so far has been negligible.

Our stock markets have been hit hard on account of political uncertainties. It is time that major political parties rise above petty politics and give the country a common minimum economic programme. They should take a cue from nations like Italy, France and Japan where governments come and go frequently, but their economic policies continue. This phenomenon has made these countries major economic powers today.

There are plenty of temptations for financial journalists to accept gifts and jaunts from corporates. In fact, the image of corporate reporters has been tarnished in recent times due to their succumbing to such offers. My advice to them is to resist such allurements and keep the flag of objective and independent reporting aloft. Credibility of a newspaper should not be bargained for anything. I express my gratitude to my colleagues in the Investor's Guide of *The Economic Times* who gave me all the help to write this book.

S.K. Aggarwal

Contents

called in one or more calls. The amount of capital paid up at any point of time is known as the paid-up capital.

Again, while an investor may apply for, say 200 shares at a subscription price of Rs. 30, fully paid-up, he may get only, say 20 shares. The application money of the investor on the 200 shares applied is (Rs. 200 × 30 = Rs. 6,000). The company would refund the balance of Rs. 5,400 to the investor since he has been allotted shares worth Rs. 600 only.

Preference Shares

Under Companies Act, new issues of share capital can be only of two kinds only, namely:

(a) Equity share capital; and

(b) Preference share capital.

Under Section 85 of Companies Act, "preference share capital" means with reference to any company limited by shares, whether formed before or after the commencement of this Act, that part of the share capital of the company which fulfils both the following requirements, namely:

(a) that in respect of dividends, it carries or will carry a preferential right to be paid a fixed amount or an amount calculated at a fixed rate, which may be either free of or subject to income-tax deductions; and

(b) that in respect of capital, it carries or will carry, on a winding up or repayment of capital, a preferential right to be repaid the amount of capital paid up or deemed to have been paid up whether or not there is preferential right to the payment of either or both of the following amounts, namely:

   (i) any money remaining unpaid, in respect of the amounts specified in clause (a) up to the date of the winding up or repayment of capital; and

   (ii) any fixed premium or premium on any fixed scale, specified in the memorandum of articles of the company.

"Equity share capital" means, with reference to any such company all shares which is not preference share capital.

A preference share is one where the preference shareholder gets preference over the ordinary shareholder. Unltil the preference shareholder has received his payment, the ordinary shareholder cannot be paid. On account of this preference over the ordinary shareholder, the preference shareholder assumes lesser risk than the former. Usually, the rate of dividend for preference share is fixed at the time of issue.

What is a Company?

A company is a form of business organisation. It is basically an association of individuals called 'shareholders' who get together for the purpose of running a particular business. The company is managed by a board of directors which consists mostly of promoters as well as elected representatives of the shareholders. The money that a company raises for starting and running its business is called *Capital*. This is initially raised from the shareholders, who jointly own the company.

In the Companies Act, "company means a company formed and registered under this Act or an existing company as defined in clause (II). The "existing company" means a company formed and registered under any of the previous companies laws. Under the law there are "private company" and "public company". The private company means a company which by its articles:

(a) restricts the right to transfer its shares, if any;
(b) limits the number of its members to fifty, not including—
  (i) persons who are in the employment of the company; and
  (ii) persons who, having been formerly in the employment of the company, were members of the company while in that employment and have continued to be members after the employment ceased; and
(c) prohibits any invitations to the public to subscribe for any shares in, or debentures of, the company.

"The Public company" means a company that is not a private company.

In short, there are two types of companies, the private companies which restrict membership to fifty and they do not raise funds in the form of shares or debentures from the public and; public companies which have no limit on the number of members and invite public to subscribe to its equity and debt instruments.

The amount so raised is called the equity capital of the company. Companies also raise capital by borrowing from the public, banks and from other financial institutions. They raise money from the public either through fixed deposits or by selling debentures. The persons who buy debentures are called debenture holders. Debenture holders are creditors of the company. They are owed money by the company, whereas shareholders are owners of the company.

The Liabilities and Rights of Shareholders

A company has an independent legal existence of its own, quite distinct from that of its shareholders. This means that the company can, without in any way involving its shareholders enter into contracts, buy, sell and own property, engage in litigation and incur debts. Shareholders cannot be held responsible for the actions of the company or any of its directors or employees. The liability of the shareholders to the company is limited to the face value of the share he holds in the company. If a company has not called full amount, shareholder is liable to pay the balance.

The worst that can happen to the shareholder is if the company becomes bankrupt and goes under liquidation the value of his share may fall to zero. Under no circumstances can a shareholder be asked to pay more money to the creditors of the company. This is the essence of the concept of limited liability. The shares are a moveable property. They can be transferred, sold, gifted and bequeathed.

There are two types of companies, public limited and private limited. It's mandatory for the private limited company to end its name with the words 'private limited', while a public limited company simply ends its name with the word limited'. When we talk of investment in shares, we are actually referring to investment in the shares of public limited companies. Shares of private limited companies are neither quoted on the stock exchange, nor are they freely available for sale. The shares of the private limited companies are held by the owner's family members and his friends or associates with maximum number of holders to fifty.

Rights Shares

Companies often require additional fund for their working capital or for their expansion. They sometimes raise these funds by the sale of additional equity shares on a rights basis to its shareholders. They are called *rights shares* because shareholders by virtue of their existing share-holding have a prior right to buy these shares. The number of rights shares offered to each shareholder is directly proportionate to the number of equity shares he owns.

Such further shares shall be offered to the persons who, at the date of offer, are holders of equity shares of the company, in proportion, as nearly as circumstances admit, to the capital paid-up on those shares at that date. Unless the articles of the company otherwise provide, the offer aforesaid shall be deemed to include a right exercisable by the person concern to renounce the shares offered to him or any of them in favour of any other person. Thus if one does not have funds or decides to renounce his right in favour of some one else he is permitted by law to do so as a matter of right.

When such shares are offered for sale at their face value, they are said to be offered at par and when the sale price is higher, they are said to be offered at a premium. Premium is the difference between the issue price of the share and its face value. In order to make the rights issue attractive, the price of rights shares is generally fixed at a level far below the prevailing market price of the company's share. The issue of rights shares increases the equity capital of the company.

Bonus Issue

When we invest the share capital in a business, we do so with the expectation of getting back not only our invested capital, but also a proportionate share of the surplus generated from operations after all the other shareholders have been paid their dues. Thus, collectively the business owes its shareholders their invested capital as well as the surplus generated from operations. But, in reality, while the business may pay us annual dividends, seldom is the surplus fully distributed as dividends. This surplus which is retained in the business is still owned by shareholders. The retained surplus is also reflected as retained earnings or reserve in the balance sheet of the company. Together, share capital and reserves are known as equity or the net worth of a company.

Over a period of time, the retained earnings of a firm can become quite large often, several times the original share capital. When this happens, the management of the firm may decide to transfer some amount from the reserve account to the share capital account by a mere book entry. This has the effect of decreasing or debiting the reserve in the balance sheet of the firm and increasing or crediting the share capital. In such a case, the firm is said to have made a bonus issue.

The issue of bonus shares should lead to a fall in the market price of a share. This does not, however, affect the shareholder adversely because this fall in the market price is more than offset by increase in the size of his share holdings.

To illustrate how this happens, let us assume that you own 100 shares in ABC Ltd., when it issues bonus shares in the ratio of 1:1. Let us also assume that the market price of the share is Rs. 50 per share prior to the bonus issue. With the issue of bonus shares your shareholding doubles to 200 shares. At the same time, market price of the shares should probably fall to Rs. 25 per share. Even though the price falls one does not lose because the value of shareholding remains at Rs. 5,000. The fall in price from Rs. 50 to Rs. 25 is fully compensated by the increase in your shareholding from 100 to 200 shares. Often price do not fall in proportion to bonus issue and thus one generally stands to gain.

Company usually continue to pay the same rate of dividend after the issue of bonus shares as they were paying prior to the issue. This benefits the shareholder because he gets the same rate of dividend on a large shareholding. A company will not normally issue bonus share unless it is confident that its future growth prospects justify an expansion in its equity capital. Therefore, the expectation of a bonus issue by any company creates a climate of optimism and cheer in the share markets. This usually results in a rise in the price of company's shares just before or on the announcement by it of a bonus issue.

The Stock Exchange

The stock exchange is basically a market-place for purchase and sale of shares and securities. That is why it is also called a stock market. Just like any other market, it brings together the potential buyers and sellers of securities. The term security is a broad generic term covering equity shares, preference shares, debentures, bonds issued by the government, semi-government and local authorities and mutual funds faded securities.

Unlike other markets, investors are not permitted to buy or sell shares directly in a stock exchange. According to the stock exchange rules, one has to do buying and selling through a licensed member of the stock exchange called a stockbroker or sharebroker or licensed sub-broker. He is authorised to buy and sell shares on behalf of others on a commission basis which is called brokerage.

The prices at which shares are bought and sold are determined by a publicly held auction on the floor of the stock exchange, called trading hall. But now transactions are also conducted on some exchanges through computers like NSE and OCTEI. Companies are required to enlist their securities with a particular stock exchange to be eligible for trading.

Trading Lot and Odd Lot

Shares are bought and sold in trading lots. A trading lot is a unit consisting of a specified number of shares which can be bought and sold in individual transactions on the stock exchange. Transactions take place in trading lots, or in multiples of trading lots. The trading lot for each company is fixed by the stock exchange and it varies from company to company. Generally, the trading lot is fixed at 100 shares or 50 shares when the face value of the share is Rs. 10 and 5 shares if the face value of the share is 100. The purpose of fixing trading lots is to provide for greater convenience and facility in stock market transactions.

The term 'Odd Lot' refers to units of shares which do not neatly add up to a trading lot. For example, if you possess 8, 12 or 19 shares of ABC Ltd., your holding would consist of an odd lot of shares. Odd lots are also bought and sold in the stock markets, but with far greater difficulty and at a slightly lower price.

Good and Bad Deliveries

Transfer of securities from one owner to the other must be accompanied by a suitable transfer deed. The terms, good and bad deliveries refer to the transfer deeds and the security certificates. In order to be good, all transfer deeds are certified either by the company or the stock exchange concerned. The transfer deed contains such information as the full name and address of the transferor and the distinctive number of the securities and the signatures of transferor or his authorised attorney. (The number printed on the certificate, the date of certification etc.) The transfer deeds must be for the exact amount of trading unit, whether marked lot or odd lot. The stamp duty and the transfer fees which is half a percent of the market price is paid by the buyer. When any of the above conditions are missing from a transfer deed, or signatures of transferor do not tally with the specimen signatures with the company the delivery is called 'Bad'.

A delivery will also be considered bad if the accompanying share certificates are mutilated, the name or the distinctive numbers are not legible, the particulars in the transfer deed do not tally with the particulars in the share certificate, the person signing the transfer deed does so on behalf of a minor or a lunatic or against whom insolvency proceedings are outstanding, if the transfer deed contains significant correction, erasure, over-writing or crossing out or change of various particulars; if the transfer deed is endorsed before the book closure but delivered after the book close; in the case of partly paid-up shares or debentures if the delivery is made after the last date for paying the call money, etc.

When share certificates are torn or mutilated, one may acquire a new certificate from the company by paying an appropriate renewal fee. The payment of stamp duty on shares transfer is uniform throughout India.

Kerb Trading

Transactions are carried out in the stock exchange after official trading hours too, even though such trading is not legal. Such unofficial trading carried out outside the stock exchange premises is known as kerb trading. Kerb trading accounts for a sizable percentage of total trading in the Indian stock exchanges. In addition, owing to the relatively weak mechanism of control in the stock exchanges, frequently some of the significant transactions carried out during the official transaction hours may not be reported by the brokers to the stock exchange authorities. The kerb prices are even quoted in some of the newspapers.

Underwriting of Issues

Making public issue of securities is risky. There is always a chance that the issue may not be fully subscribed, though this chance may be high or low depending upon the size of the issue, the track record of the company/promoters making the issue, the nature of project for which the issue is having made, the general economic and political conditions, etc.

Companies would like to save themselves of this worry and attend to their operations whole-heartedly if they could have someone else to worry on their behalf. In other words, they would like to have their issues *underwritten*. This service is provided by underwriters. The underwriters undertake to buy the stock under issue to the extent they are not fully subscribed by the public. The underwriters may be large brokers, merchant bankers, banks, financial institutions/ mutual funds. They insure stocks against non-subscription.

Debenture

A debenture represents the smallest unit of public lending to a company. Like share, they are also represented in the form of a certificate. The common face value for a debenture in India is Rs. 100 and they are issued at par. Debentureholders do not have voting right. Unlike an ordinary shareholder, a debenture holder assumes very little risk in his investment. Unlike the uncertain stream of dividends which a shareholder receives, a debentureholder receives a fixed rate of interest. Payment of such interest is a legal obligation on the part of the company, but when there is liquidity crisis in the company there one defaults.

Further, in general, a debenture is required to be secured against the assets of the company. Thus, a debenture is a form of secured loan. Secured debenture implies that should a company default in its obligations towards debentureholders in the payment of interest and the principal, the assets of the company can be sold off towards realising the dues of the debentureholders.

The debentureholders are investors who assume relatively little risk on their investment and accordingly the returns are lower than that of ordinary shareholders. Debentureholders are lenders of funds and not owners, they therefore, do not enjoy any voting rights, except under exceptional circumstances. Unlike dividend, interest on debentures is deductable from the corporate profits and is treated as a business expense.

Debentures are essentially of three kinds, Fully convertible (FCD) Partly convertible (PCD) and Non-convertible (NCD).

Fully convertible debenture (FCD): A fully convertible debenture is a debenture which at a specified time after the issue, is fully converted to equity shares.

Partly convertible debenture (PCD): A partly convertible debenture is one only a part of which is convertible into an ordinary share. For example, a debenture priced at Rs. 100 may have two components, namely, a convertible component A and non-convertible component B priced at Rs. 30 and Rs. 70, respectively. Here only component A priced at Rs. 30 is convertible into an ordinary share while the non-convertible component B priced at Rs. 70 is allowed to remain intact.

Non-Convertible Debenture (NCD): These debentures cannot be converted into ordinary shares. These debentures may be redeemable at a premium. They may also be irredeemable or perpetual. In India, the interest rate on non-convertible debentures paid by the companies is usually 2 to 2.5% higher than that for convertible debentures.

Under the Sebi guidelines, conversion must take place at or after 18 months at the option of the debentureholder. The guidelines also require that all debentures with conversion or maturity over 18 months be credit rated and that the premium amount at the time of conversion, the redemption amount, period of maturity and yield on redemption time be indicated in the prospectus.

Bonds

A bond is more or less the same as a debenture. In India, the terms bonds and debentures are mostly used interchangeably. There is virtually no distinction between the two and the difference, if any, is subtle enough to be disregarded for all practical purposes.

Zero Coupon Bond or Deep Discount Bond

A zero coupon bond or a deep discount bond is a loan instrument slightly different from an ordinary debenture. Unlike an ordinary debenture which is usually offered at its face value (say Rs. 100) and earns interest till redemption (say 15 per cent per annum) and is redeemed with or without premium. A five year zero coupon bond may be offered at a discount (say at Rs. 50) and fetches no periodic interest and is redeemed at the face value (say Rs. 100). A little computation reveals that the *yield to maturity* or YTM of such a zero coupon bond when subscribed to at Rs. 50 is about 15 per cent which is similar to that of an ordinary debenture subscribed to at face value which is redeemed without premium. It is simply that instead of receiving the interest periodically, the bondholder receives the principal as well as compounded interest together at the time of maturity of the bond. In other words, the interest is automatically reinvested at 15 per cent per annum till maturity.

The implication of such an instrument in India may be of significance to the investors in the high-tax brackets, depending upon whether or not they can treat the implicit interest accrued at the time of redemption as capital gains. Since the interest on the bonds is received only at the time of redemption, it is allowed to be accounted for as premium at redemption attracting capital gains tax rather than income tax, the bonds may have special attraction (since the capital gains tax rate is generally lower than the income tax rate).

Recently convertible zero coupon bonds have been issued in the Indian capital market. These all zero coupon bonds, which, instead of being redeemed, are converted into ordinary shares.

Bulls, Bears and Stags

Those who buy shares in anticipation of increase in prices are commonly referred to as *bulls*. Those who sell shares anticipating a fall in prices are referred to as *bears*. The *stags* are those who in general do not invest in the secondary market. Instead, they prefer to make their investments in the primary market when new issues are made. So a bullish market implies a rising market, since that is when the *bulls,* or the buyers, enter the field. Similarly, a bearish market is the falling market, attracting the *bears,* or the sellers. Also, the same individual may play the bull's role with one security, and a *bear's* role with another, as he may be anticipating the price of the former security to rise and that of the latter to fall. Traditionally, stock exchanges have been a male preserve. Hence the choice of male animals.

Spot Trading

Under the spot basis of trading, the seller of a share must deliver the share certificate within 48 hours to the buying broker. As such, the seller receives the selling price immediately upon the delivery of the shares. Thus, under this basis of trading, delivery of security certificate and payment of cash are more or less immediate.

Cash Basis of Trading

Notwithstanding the term 'cash basis', the securities are not exactly traded for cash. In general, actual delivery of certificates and the payment of cash must take place before the next settlement date meant for cash transactions, when outstanding accounts arising from the cash basis of trading among the brokers are settled. Since the settlement date for cash transactions occurs only once in two weeks in most stock exchanges in India (different stock exchanges have their settlement on different days of alternate weeks), the cash or certificates mostly change hands only on the following settlement date after the deal is made. Further, the certificates have to be registered in the name of the buyer in the company's records. For this purpose, the seller executes a transfer deed, which attracts a nominal stamp fee of Re. 0.50 per Rs. 100 worth of shares to be borne by the buyer. This transfer deed is delivered to the buyer, who in turn, sends the deed and the share certificate to the company for effecting the change of name in their records. Unfortunately in India, this process can often take up to four months and sometimes even more, though under the law, it should be closed within 45 days.

Settlement or Badla Trading

Under the spot and cash basis of trading, a share can be bought only if we have adequate money, or sold only if we have the requisite share certificates. However, under settlement trading (also commonly referred to as *Badla trading*, or *Vayada trading* and sometimes incorrectly as forward trading), it is possible to buy shares, even if we do not have the requisite amount of money, or sell shares even if we do not have the share certificates.

Let us suppose that we want to buy a promising security so that when its price has risen sufficiently we may sell it for a profit. But we do not have the money to buy it. Therefore, we raise a loan to buy it. In future, if the price of the share does increase as anticipated, we can sell off the share and repay the loan along with interest. Thus, the increase in the price of the share minus the interest on the borrowing will be our profit. However, if the price goes down contrary to our expectation, we suffer a loss.

Similarly, when we anticipate the price of a share to go down in future, we borrow a share certificate and sell it. When, in future, the price falls as anticipated by us, we buy the share at the reduced price and return it to the lender of the share certificate, along with some charge for the borrowing. Thus, the fall in the price of the share minus the borrowing charge for the share certificate will be our profit. If, however, the share price goes up contrary to our expectations, we suffer a loss.

While this system facilitates buying and selling of shares without payment of cash or delivery of shares at short notice, the *badla* system had led to accumulation of payments and frequent defaults. Consequently, the stock exchange had to shut down to find out ways to settle the payments and ensure the delivery of share certificates. Sebi banned the *badla* system in March 1994.

Forward Delivery

It is a transaction entered into for delivery on Payment in future. In the case of forward delivery contracts, the settlement is made on a fixed day, may be once a week or once a fortnight. If the transaction could not be carried, then there is a system of 'carry over' to the next settlement if agreed upon by the two parties. If the buyer desires to carry over, he has to pay a premium or consideration to the seller known as *Contango*. But if the seller desires to carry over, he pays a premium to the buyer known as *backwardation*.

Group A and B Shares

Shares listed on the stock exchanges are normally divided into two distinct categories: Cleared securities and non-cleared securities. The current practice is to refer to cleared securities as Group A shares or specified shares and non-cleared securities as Group B shares.

Transactions in Group A shares are settled between members through the 'clearing house' attached to a stock exchange. This clearing house performs virtually the same functions as the clearing house of a bank. Settlement in cleared securities is done every fortnight. During settlement, the purchase and sales of Group A shares is made by the various members during the fortnight are adjusted by means of book transfers and they are required to pay or receive payment only for the net amounts which remains unadjusted. The transactions in Group B shares are not settled through the clearing house of the stock exchange. Members settle transactions in such shares directly with each other.

The most actively traded shares are normally included in the Group A category—this category includes the biggest and the most well-known companies. In India, speculation is mostly confined to Group A shares.

Blue Chips

There is no standard definition of 'blue chips'. It is a term loosely used for companies that are sound in every respect. Companies that are large in size, technologically advanced, have professional management of high calibre, and have built up a reputation for growth, regular payment of high dividends, and integrity in business dealings would normally be qualified to be labelled as blue chips.

BSE Sensitive Index

This is popularly used stock as market index in India. The purpose of a stock market index is to provide a means for measuring the trends in share prices. The BSE sensitive Index, popularly known as the 'Sensex' was first constructed in 1876 with 1876-79 as the base year. The value of the Sensex in the base year is taken to be 100. The Sensex is composed of 30 scrips selected on the basis of their size and daily trading volume. Each scrip is given weightage on the basis of the market capitalisation (number of equity shares multiplied by the share price). The Sensex was revised from August 19, 1996. The index is extremely sensitive to changes in the share prices of the larger companies. The names of the companies included in the index are given below:

1. Bajaj Auto
2. Mahindra & Mahindra
3. Telco
4. ACC
5. Gujarat-Ambuja Cement
6. Reliance Industries Ltd.
7. Hindustan Petroleum Corpn. Ltd.
8. Tata Chem
9. IPCL
10. Grasim Industries
11. Ranbaxy Laboratories Ltd.
12. Glaxo India Ltd.
13. Arvind Mills
14. Hindustan Levers Ltd.
15. ITC Ltd.
16. Nestle Ltd.
17. Colgate
18. TISCO
19. SAIL
20. Hindalco
21. Larsen & Toubro
22. BHEL
23. Tata Power
24. BSES Ltd.
25. MTNL
26. SBI
27. IDBI
28. ICCI
29. Indian Hotel
30. Great Eastern Shipping

Excessive Speculation and How to Curb It

Some amount of speculation is always present in the market and not all speculations are unhealthy for the market. It is only when the speculation becomes dominant that it begins to cause serious concern. In such cases, the stock exchange authorities usually detect the excessive speculation in a particular security at any time through wide fluctuations in its price. This is because unusual fluctuations in a particular security are linked to extraordinary interest by somebody in that security.

For example, if someone is buying large quantities of a particular share, the price of that share is bound to go up steeply, since the demand increases while the supply of the share remains the same. Similarly, if somebody is selling a large number of a particular share, the price is bound to fall sharply, since the supply of the shares increases in relation to its demand.

Sometimes there may be unusual buying or selling activity in the share of a company on account of *inside information,* such as a company's plan to enter into profitable collaboration with another company. The fact is bound to be known to some senior members of the company's management much ahead of the public. Thus, based on this *inside information,* such members may indulge in heavy speculative buying of their company's shares. Since in these cases the volume of individual transactions often tend to be rather large, the fluctuation in share prices in such situations tend to be larger. This kind of trading based on *inside information* is also known as *insider trading*. When such *insider trading* is on the rise, a few individuals with superior inside information tend to make large fortunes at the cost of the common investors.

In the absence of adequate laws restricting *inside trading,* it has become too common. Our financial institutions like the Unit Trust of India and the general insurance companies hold massive investments in the corporate sector. These institutions are represented on the boards of the companies. It is possible that these institutions indulge in *inside trading,* especially since they have their own pressures for performance, which is mainly profitability. Similarly senior staff members and management can also do so.

The stocks made available to the public are inadequate. Nearly 35 per cent of the shares are held by the financial institutions and another 30 to 35 per cent are closely held by the controlling groups, only the residual of about 30 per cent are available to the public. It is reasonable to believe that given the increasing public interest in the capital market in recent years, the shares availability to the public is far from adequate. When financial institutions decide to buy or sell thousands of shares of any one company at a time, the big changes in the supply and demand of the shares add to the fluctuations in the share prices.

The situation is further compounded by government encouragement on multiple listing of a share (the requirement that share be listed in more than one stock exchange) which instead of active trading of the shares, scatters the already limited stock of floating demand in relation to supply of stocks leading to price imbalances.

The stock exchange authorities have a variety of measures in their arsenal to choose from, whenever they perceive the price movements in the market to be unusually high, indicating excessive speculation, with possibility of high default risk. To begin with, they may impose a *daily margin* on the settlement trading (and sometimes even on the cash trading) of the concerned security. The margin may be a percentage of the share price, or simply the absolute amount on each share. It may be levied on the bulls as well as bears, *i.e.* on both buy and sell transactions. Imposition of daily margin requires the buyer or the seller, as the case may be, to deposit the margin money with the stock exchange authorities (through the broker) on the basis of the extent of transaction being done by him every day. For example, if the daily margin on a particular security is 10 per cent on the price of that security, a buyer of that security in the carry-forward market has to pay the margin amount to his broker in order to have his order executed. The higher the suspected degree of speculation, the higher the margin. The margin acts as an insurance against possible default risk of the speculations and also reduces the degree of speculation.

There may also be a *carry-over margin,* which is levied only if a transaction is carried forward to the next settlement period. The purpose of the carry-over margin is to discourage indiscriminate carrying forward of transactions and induce the speculators to settle at least part of their transactions through actual deliveries or paying the difference between buying rates and carry-over rates. Daily margins and carry-over margins may also be levied simultaneously. Clearly, the requirement of margin discourages the participation of reckless speculators who may be speculating beyond their means.

The stock exchange authorities may also influence the settlement price itself so as to reduce the default risk in the market. For example, let us assume that a particular high-priced security has risen steeply during a settlement period, say from Rs. 1,400 to Rs. 2,150 and a large volume, say 20,000 of this share, has been sold by one party to another during a settlement period. Now, if the settlement price were fixed at Rs. 2,150, the seller will be called to pay the price difference of Rs. 1.50 crore (Rs. 750 × 20,000). Since such a transaction being carried forward may in all likelihood be speculative, the Executive Director of the exchange may decide to keep the settlement price lower, say Rs. 1,800.

Recourse Available to Investors Regarding Their Grievances

The complaints of investors against companies typically relate to:

(a) late or non-receipt of refund order,
(b) late or non-receipt of allotment letter,
(c) late or non-receipt of share certificate,
(d) delay in transfer of securities,
(e) odd lots,
(f) late or non-payment of interest on debentures,
(g) late or non-payment of principal on redemption, etc.

The Companies Act, 1956 provides for several in-built protection measures for investors in virtually all the above cases. For instance, according to the Companies Act, a company is obliged to refund the oversubscribed amount within 8 days of the amount becoming due for refund. Similarly, the stock exchanges division of the Ministry of Finance, Government of India directs the companies to make such refunds within two months of the closure of the subscription list. Failure on the part of the company to do so can attract a penal interest payment up to 15 per cent per annum for delays over 60 days. Again, the refunds and allotment orders, etc., are required to be despatched by registered post by the companies as an additional safeguard for the investors.

Similarly, under normal circumstances, the Companies Act provides for every company to despatch security certificates within 3 months of allotment. A failure to comply with the above requirements can attract fine up to Rs. 500 per day of default. The investor is also free to launch criminal proceedings against the company. Similarly, Companies Act provides for a company to effect transfer of securities within two months of their being delivered to the company.

Under the Securities Contracts (Regulation) Act, 1956, a company can refuse to effect transfer of shares only if the instrument is improper or lacking in formal details of registration, etc., or if the transfer is for some reasons unlawful, or likely to result in a change in the composition of the board of directors. In case of perfect transfer deed refusal requires approval of Company Law Board. Regarding difficulties in trading of odd lot shares, the stock exchanges division of the Government of India directs the stock exchanges to advise the companies to effect the consolidation and issue of certificates in market lots when odd lot shares adding up to market lots are delivered for transfer. Companies are also advised to make pro-active moves in offering to encash the odd lot holdings of their shareholders. These odd lots are then converted into marketable lots in the names of such nominees as may be assigned by the stock exchanges. Various mutual funds, such as, Canbank Financial Services Ltd., General Insurance Corporation and Unit Trust of India, offer odd lot trading services to their investors.

Most of these schemes take the shape of across-the-counter trading for a designated securities on specific days and times for a nominal 2 per cent to 3 per cent commission at the previous day's closing quotations. You can get the requisite information from the nearest offices of these organisations.

As far as the delays in payments of dividends, etc. are concerned, if they have been declared but not been paid, the Companies Act provides prosecution of the directors. The investor may also take recourse to initiating criminal proceedings against the erring company.

It is evident that while the law does protect the investor and provides for certain deterrents, in reality the deterrents often turn out to be incentives. For example, a penal interest rate of 15 per cent or less is hardly punitive when the borrowing rate in the market is closer to 20 per cent. Similarly, a fine of Rs. 500 per day for a company is hardly a deterrent. It is, therefore, scarcely surprising that notwithstanding all the legal provisions, the defaults continue to abound and investors are frequently at the mercy of the companies.

The real issue is not whether the law prohibits a certain action (or inaction) on the part of a company and provides for legal recourse. The real issue is whether or not the legal penalties are prohibitive enough to prevent these defaults from taking place in the first place. Unfortunately, they do not.

At any rate, it is also open to the investors to send their complaints to the Department of Company Affairs, the Registrar of Companies of the relevant jurisdiction, the stock exchange in which the company is listed or the Securities & Exchanges Board of India and journals. These agencies do take necessary measures in such cases, but the redress is usually quite slow. Unfortunately, the freedom to launch criminal proceedings etc. hardly offer a realistic redress to the investors.

It may be worthwhile to note that there are already several stockholders' associations active in various cities which can help redress some of the grievances of their members. Many of these associations are already recognised by the Securities and Exchanges Board of India. It would be worthwhile for serious investors to become member of at least one such association. To ensure, however, that the association you choose is recognized by Sebi and has a track record of committed work, lest you should be wasting your membership fee, and the cure should become worse than the malady.

One would also expect the financial press to become more vigilant and responsible in bringing errant participants to book. Perhaps, the industry itself should evolve certain guidelines as self-regulatory measures. It should be recognised all around, that free market regulations and self-regulation almost go hand-in-hand.

Arbitration Proceedings

The contracts made in the stock exchanges are all subject to arbitration proceedings as provided under the relevant bye-laws. Whenever a dispute arises among members, the matter may be referred to the *arbitration committee*. This is a standing committee constituted by the governing board of the stock exchange every year comprising members of the stock exchange. Presently, the government is also considering appointing of independent professionals on the Arbitration Committee.

When disputes arise between a member and one of the constituents (anyone, such as, an institution, investor, *badla* financier, a company, etc. placing an order for a transaction with a recognised member of the stock exchange) or vice versa, then each party may appoint an arbitrator who will be a member of the stock exchange. Under special circumstances, the dispute may be referred to an arbitration committee at the option of the constituents.

Normally, the disputes are resolved within four months of commencement. Also, if no arbitration proceedings are filed within three months of the origin of a dispute, the dispute becomes time-barred.

Most stock exchanges are also setting up investor protection funds which is used for compensating a genuine investor in case of default of payment or delivery of shares by a member broker of the exchange. Special officers are also being appointed in many stock exchanges to deal with investor complaints.

Again, the current penal provisions for the errant brokers for violating the prescribed norms are far too mild to be an effective deterrent. One would like to see more vigorous measures on the part of the government and stock exchange authorities on this front. On its part, the Sebi is quite apprised of this problem. In fact, most of its guidelines concerning the functioning of the securities market intermediaries are trying to keep investor protection uppermost in mind. One of the tasks before Sebi is also to promote organisations to protect investors.

In the final analysis, however, the best investor protection is the investor education. Stock market is not for the ignorant. Stock market is also not for the small investors, they should seek the refuge of mutual funds, without attempting to negotiate the quick sands of stock market on their own.

Portfolio

The set of all securities held by an investor is called his *portfolio*. The portfolio may contain just one security. However, since in general no one puts one's all eggs in one basket, it will contain several securities, such as shares, debentures, government bonds, Unit Trust and other mutual funds, certificates and other financial assets.

Stock Holding Corporation of India Limited or SHCIL

The SHCIL would be a corporation holding stocks on behalf of investors. To begin with, the Corporation's activities are to be limited to the holdings of financial institutions, banks and mutual funds only. However, presently even individual investors are proposed to be covered through the brokers. The National Clearance and Depository System (NCDS) operated by the SHCIL is aimed at improving the operation of the Indian stock market, by overcoming the 'paper-work'.

Our manual systems of clearing and settlement of transactions, transfer and registration of securities etc. have become increasingly sluggish in the face of the phenomenal growth in capital markets in the last few years. These systems while they have served us well, have now gone weak. The market is so increasingly being subjected to delays, frauds, defaults and various other infractions of large proportions that the systemic risk in the market has gone up substantially in recent times. We cannot hope to join the mainstream of world markets with outdated systems.

These compulsions have triggered the need for the National Clearance and Depository System, a fully computerized system of clearing, settlement, which will not only do away with the manual systems, but also dispense with the antiquated system of physical transfer of shares, which itself is the primary cause of much of our stock market malady. NCDS, when operational, it is hoped will bring down the cost of clearing and settlement of transactions and transfer of shares, speed up the processes manifold, reduce problem of bad debtors, reduce the systemic risk associated with the clearing and settlement processes in our capital market, meet international standards, provide credibility to the Indian stock market in the world markets; pave the way for other related financial services to develop and all in all hasten the overall development of the Indian capital market.

The exact modalities of its operation will be known only after the system becomes fully operational. Broadly, however, the SHCIL in due course is expected to result in centralization of all clearing, settlement, and share registration and transfer functions at one point, much in the manner of a bank acting as a central clearing house for cheques.

The Parliament has cleared the Bill for the setting up of depository. It would be operational soon.

Nikkei Index

Nikkei Index is the most widely quoted measure of stock price movement on the Tokyo Stock Exchange, the world's second biggest in terms of market capitalisation. Strictly, the Nikkei measure is not an index but an average of 225 shares, and is not weighed according to each component share's market capitalisation. This means that the movement in the shares of smaller firms can move the index as much as those of big ones. The Nikkei index is run by *Nihon Keizai Shimbun,* Japan's main financial daily newspaper (Nikkei is a Japanese abbreviation of the paper's name) and was known as the Nikkei-Don Jones average until Don Jones pulled out in 1985.

Wall Street

The Wall Street is the symbol of capitalism, the street runs a third of a mile in lower Manhattan. The Wall Street remains New York's financial heart with plenty of skyscrappers tall enough for bankrupt financiers to end it all after a stock market crash. The world's biggest and oldest Stock Exchange, the New York Stock Exchange (founded in 1792) is located in Wall Street.

Dalal Street

Like Wall Street in USA, Dalal Street in India is symbol of capital market. The oldest stock exchange, *i.e.* Bombay Stock Exchange is situated on this street and many brokers offices are in and around this street. A financial journal has also been started by the name of Dalal Street Journal.

Jobbers

In the developed countries, brokers have long since graduated to rendering a whole range of consulting and advisory services to their clients based on their own research and analysis. Unfortunately, the profession of brokers in India has remained by and large a rather closed club, traditional and primitive. Their function has largely remained limited to carrying out the transaction orders on behalf of their clients (and often at prices far from satisfactory). *Jobbers* are sub-brokers or a broker's broker, or one who specialises in specific securities catering to the needs of other brokers, their activities are less organized and regulated.

Efforts are being made to professionalise the services of brokers through various means. For example, the BSE has set up a full-fledged training college to develop the professional standards of its members as well as investors. Other institutions like the various Indian Institutes of Management (IIMS), Institutes of Chartered Financial Analysts of India, Unit Trust of India, etc. have also started to play a useful part in professionalising the discipline of investment analysis. Also, there is an increasing trend to admit qualified professionals as members of the exchanges. Corporate membership to stock exchanges has already been introduced. So over a period of time, we can reasonably hope that the service would get increasingly professionalised.

Primary and Secondary Markets

A company cannot easily find takers for its securities (shares or debentures) from the public if they cannot subsequently trade these shares and debentures at will. In other words, a security cannot have a good primary market unless it has an active secondary market.

Primary market comprises the companies making the security issues, and the public at large subscribing to them. Primary market is where a company makes its first contact with the public at large in search of capital. Therefore, if one is wondering whether or not to invest in the new issue of a company, one is contemplating whether or not to participate in the primary market.

Secondary market comprises the buyers and sellers of shares and debentures subsequent to the original issue. For example, having subscribed to the share or debenture of a company, if one wishes to sell the same, it will be done in the secondary market. Similarly, one could also buy the shares or debentures of a company from the secondary market (if the company is listed in the stock exchange).

The two markets mentioned above are not to be understood as two physically segregated institutions. Often the same parties may be involved in both the markets. Primary market merely alludes to the first investment in new shares or debentures by the public directly from the issuing company, whereas secondary market refers to the subsequent trading in those shares and debentures. A stock exchange is the single most important institution in the secondary market for securities.

Prospectus

A prospectus is a document that must accompany the application forms of all public issues of securities, whether ordinary shares, preference shares, or debentures. Typically, a prospectus contains the terms and conditions of the issue, alongwith the specific feature of the security, the purpose for which the issue is being made, the company's track record, the risks inherent in the project for which the capital is being raised, addresses of directors, extract of major contracts and relevant information of the project and purpose for which funds are being raised. The specific features of the security being issued may include such details as whether the security is redeemable or irredeemable, cumulative or non-cumulative, convertible or non-convertible, secured or unsecured, is with or without warrant, etc. and such other information as the date of conversion, exercise price, redemption, interest rate, premium at redemption, and so on. Sebi has also laid out certain guidelines for the information content of a prospectus and before issue of prospectus it has to be veted by Sebi. Misleading or false information in the prospectus can attract penal actions.

Under the Companies Act 'prospectus' means any document described or issued as a prospectus and includes any notice, circular, advertisement or other document inviting deposits from public or inviting offers from the public for the subscription or purchase of any shares or debentures of a body corporate. The Act has laid down what matters have to be stated and reports set out in prospectus. This is an important document and should be studied carefully before making a decision to subscribe. There are cases when full information has not been revealed to the public inspite of veting by Sebi.

Book Closure and Record Dates

An important aspect of investing in securities is to understand the purpose and implications of book closure or record date.

Since the securityholders of a company keep changing practically everyday, when a company has to distribute benefits in the form of interest, dividends, bonus shares or rights issues, the company has to ascertain as to who should receive the benefits. For this purpose, for each benefit to be distributed to the securityholders, a company announces in advance a record/book closure date. The benefits are then distributed to those securityholders whose names appear on the register of the company on that date. To receive this benefit from the company, an investor who has bought the security on a cum-benefit basis, must make sure that the security is sent for transfer to his name before the book closure date.

This date also has an implication for the validity of the transfer deed which accompanies a security certificate. A certificate is accompanied with a transfer deed, signed by the seller, renouncing his right to the certificate in favour of the buyer. These transfer deeds are date stamped, and are valid only till the next book closure date. If the certificate is not sent for transfer before the next book closure date, a fresh transfer deed, dated after the book closure is required for the transfer. An investor has to be, therefore, particular about whether the transaction has been done on cum-benefit or ex-benefit basis and what the book closure date is for the distribution of the benefit, otherwise he may miss the benefit and sometimes also go through considerable difficulty in getting new transfer deeds signed.

Price/Earnings Ratio

A useful measure of share prices, is the ratio of the market price of an ordinary share to the earnings (profits) per share. The higher the P/E ratio, the more the stock market is buying a company's shares in the expectation that it will make larger profits in future. P/E ratios, therefore, vary widely: in mid-1986, the New York stock market offered an average ratio of 15.2, while London had an average of 14.5 and Tokyo's average was a lofty 41.2.

Investors use P/E ratios to gauge whether one company's share price is too high or too low compared to its earnings and with competitors with similar products and earnings performance, or compared with past ratios. Comparisons between firms in different countries are tricky, however, because different accounting conventions produce widely divergent figures for profits and cash flow. Japanese companies, for instance, generally have P/E ratios of between 30 and 100 because earnings are understated compared with western equivalents.

FERA Companies

You will frequently come across the term 'FERA Company' in newspapers and magazines. FERA is an abbreviation which stands for the Foreign Exchange Regulation Act 1973. The provisions of this act put a number of restrictions on the operations of companies owned and controlled by foreigners. A FERA company is one in which foreigners hold more than 40 per cent of its equity capital.

Most of the Indian subsidiaries of multinational corporation are FERA companies. They constitute some of the best managed and most technologically advanced companies in India. They have a history and reputation of yielding rich returns to investors. Most of them have a record of not only giving high dividends but also liberal and frequent bonus shares to their shareholders. There are presently over 50 such companies in India, and their shares are, by and large, good investments.

Closely-Held Companies

Whether a company is widely-held or closely-held depends upon the number of shareholders it has. We will draw the line at 5,000 shareholders. Companies with less than 5,000 shareholders will be described as closely-held.

Shares of closely-held companies tend to be less active than those of widely-held ones since they have a fewer number of shareholders and thus a smaller floating stock of shares. They tend to be ignored by the general public. Large institutional investors also tend to avoid closely-held companies. As a result, their shares do not get sufficient price support which they would have otherwise got if they had been widely held. Moreover, it is always much easier to manipulate the share prices of a closely-held company than those of a widely-held one.

Share prices of closely-held companies also tend to be more volatile than others. When they rise, they rise very fast, and to a very high level. Conversely, when they fall, they fall very fast and to a very low level. As a result, it is generally very difficult to buy shares in a closely-held company when prices are rising, and very difficult to sell them when prices are falling. Investing in such shares requires a high degree of expertise and the risk factor is also high.

How to Read Daily Market Quotations?

The stock market quotations or the price at which the shares are transacted daily on the stock exchanges and are extensively covered in daily newspapers. *The Business Standard, The Economic Times, The Financial Express, The Business Line* give a more detailed coverage of the quotations. The information is given in *The Economic Times* under the following heads:

Co. Prices (Vol., Val. Rs. '000s, No. Trds) P/E 52-wk/H/L. Co. means name of the company: Bombay Dyeing (203 means previous day's closing per share). Price quotation: 200, 203, 201 indicate the three prices at which the Bombay Dyeing shares were transacted during that particular day, Volume means number of shares traded, value stands for total value of shares, No. Trds. stands for number of transactions of trading in the share, P/E means per earning ratio, 52-wk/H/L means that within a year how much a share went up and how much it fell.

Net Asset Value

If you invest in mutual funds then the most important financial indicator (or ratio) that one needs to know is Net Asset Value (NAV). The net asset value of a fund is equal to its total assets *i.e.* market value of shares + cash balance, minus operational and other expenses divided by the total number of shares issued by the fund. NAV is a very useful ratio. It tells you what each individual share issued by the fund is worth at any given point of time. For example, if the NAV of the fund is Rs. 22.35 per share on any given date then it means that if the fund were to be liquidated on that date, each share of the fund would find you a sum of Rs. 22.35.

The NAV also helps you to evaluate and keep track of fund's performance and for comparing the performance of different funds.

Badliwala

An intermediary who provides the necessary finance for taking delivery of shares or lends the required shares for making delivery at the end of a clearing is called as *'badliwala'*. He lends finance for taking delivery of securities to the market when it is short of funds for receiving delivery on the due date at the end of the clearing or settlement period for those who wish to carry over their purchases. He loans securities to the market when it is short of adequate supply of scrips by giving delivery on the due date at the end of the clearing for those who wish to carry over their sales.

Bulge

A quick temporary price rise that applies to the entire commodities or stock market, or an individual commodity or stock is called 'bulge'.

Buyer's Market

Buyer's market is another name for bear market with an excess of supply of shares over demand and consequent low prices. This is the opposite of seller's market.

Bear Market

A prolonged period of falling prices is called 'bear market'. A bear market in stocks is brought on by the anticipation of declining economic activity. Bear markets usually last from 6 to 24 months.

Alpha Shares

The most frequently traded shares, are also called specified shares, 'A' group securities, cleared securities.

Authorised Share Capital

The maximum number of shares that a company is authorised to issue is stated in the memorandum of association of the company and under the law company capital cannot be higher than this amount. It also specifies the type of capital.

Capital Asset Pricing Model (CAPM)

It explains the behaviour of security prices and provides a mechanism whereby investors could assess the impact of a proposed security investment on the overall portfolio risk and return.

Coupons

Small pieces of paper attached to bonds are called 'coupons'. They are detached off and cashed like preprinted cheques when investors collect coupon interest payments (usually payable bi-annually).

Credit Rating

Credit rating is a measurement of the ability of a company to meet its obligations, such as, secured and unsecured loans and interests, fixed deposits etc. Credit Rating Information Services of India Limited (CRISIL), Investment Information and Credit Rating Agency of India Limited (ICRA), Credit Analysis and Research (CARE) do such an evaluation at the request of the Companies accepting fixed deposits and floating secured non-convertible debentures. This is now compulsory.

The Companies are rated AAA, AA, A, BBB, BB, B, C and D in gradings depending upon how risky they are. AAA rating is for the lowest risk, whereas D signifies the most risky company, which is virtually in default. Rating A and BBB stand for adequate investment safety and BB, B, C and D are rated as speculative grade which are susceptible to default.

Fully Paid

Applied to new issues, when the total amount payable in relation to new shares has been paid to the company.

Moorat

Auspicious trading on Diwali during specified hours on the stock exchange.

New worth

1. On balance sheets, the total of equity share capital and reserves, 2. The value of the total assets minus total liabilities of a company is its net worth.

Over Bought

It refers to a security or a market that has just experienced an unexpectedly sharp price rise and is therefore vulnerable to a drop (called a correction by technical analysis). When a stock is overbought, few buyers are left to drive the price up.

Parri-Passu

Ranking equally. After conversion from debentures, the new shares created carry the same rights as the other shares of the company to receive dividends, rights and bonus shares, and to participate in the company's profit and loss as equity shareholders.

Permitted Securities

Shares of the company not listed on particular stock exchange but listed on other stock exchanges for which trading is being permitted on the stock exchange is called as 'permitted security'. A share listed on one stock exchange can be permitted share on the other.

Private Placement

The sale of an entire issue to a large investor (Life Insurance Corporation) with or without the aid of an underwriter.

Green Shoe Option

An option given to a company to retain over subscription. It is mentioned in prospectus.

Hammering the Market

Concerted selling of shares by operators to bring the prices down after heavy short-selling.

Short Covering

The act of buying stocks to cover the borrowings made by a short seller in the market.

Fundamental Analysis

Scientific study of the basis factors which determine the share's value. The analyst studies the industry and company's sales, assets, liabilities, debt structure, earnings, products, market share, evaluate company's management, compare the company with its competitors and then estimate the share's intrinsic worth. The fundamental analyst's tools are financial ratios arrived at by studying company's balance sheet and profit and loss account over a number of years.

2

Economic Terms

Ad Valorem

An indirect tax that is levied as a percentage of the price of a good or service. The revenue raised then increases with the value of the good. Examples are value added tax and most sales taxes. Customs and excise duty on many items is *'ad valorem'*. Contrast with specific duties, which are a fixed amount regardless of value, for example, £ 1.00 on a bottle of whisky whether it is the cheapest or the finest.

Amortization

Running down, or payment of a loan in instalments. Mortgages for house purchase, for instance, are 'amortized' by making regular payments over time plus interest. With loans that are not 'amortized', the borrower pays only interest during the period of the loan, and then repays the sum in full.

Balance of Payments

Politically sensitive record of a country's transactions in goods, services and money with other countries and with international institutions. A country's balance of payments has two accounts, current and capital: by definition, the two must balance. The most widely quoted is the current account.

Current Account

On the current account appear:

'Visible' Trade—known as merchandise trade—imports and exports of goods.

'Invisible' Trade—payments and receipts for services, such as shipping, insurance, banking, tourism, plus dividend and interest payments.

Private transfers—such as remittances from migrant workers, for example, Turks and Yugoslavs working in West Germany, or Mexicans in America or Keralites working in the Gulf.

Official transfers—such as debt interest or payments to

international organisations (for example, contributions from Britain to the EEC budget). Sometimes, however, the current account is shown net of official transfers.

Balance Sheet

A snapshot of a company's financial position at any one moment, it measures wealth, but no income; profit and loss are measured in a separate account. Normally published once a year in the annual report, or quarterly if national law requires it. Most of the companies issue their balance sheets as on 31st March but few have their balance sheets as on 31st December.

A balance sheet provides details of Liabilities, which normally include: issued share capital (that is, money provided by shareholders) reserves, balance of profit & loss, mortgages, loan capital, debenture stock; capital reserves; current liabilities including bank overdrafts, unpaid taxes, debts owed to suppliers. It includes assets, which are fixed (factories, buildings, machinery and so on) or financial (cash in hand, office items such as, stocks, work in progress and short term loans that can be quickly turned into cash, and money owed by customers). By definition the two sides balance.

Bank for International Settlements (BIS)

The central bankers' Central Bank, was founded in Basle in 1930. It has 29 shareholders, and a board representing the 13 leading central banks. The BIS has three main functions.

1. As banker, accepting deposits from its member central banks (which it then holds in short-dated paper), and making loans on their behalf. One example: through the BIS, the leading industrial countries lent the International Monetary Fund $ 1 billion in May 1981 to supplement the IMF's lending capacity. The BIS also lent money to Hungary, Mexico and Brazil in 1982, when they were unable to borrow what they needed from commercial banks.
2. It acts clearing house on questions, such as, the supervision of the Euromarkets. By pooling information on banks operating in their countries, members build up a world-wide picture of banks' lending and deposit practices and can then try to ensure that they stick to prudential guidelines.

3. It functions as a pressure group, promoting the central bank's view on both domestic and international questions. This is usually done discreetly (the BIS has a reputation for being one of the world's most tight-lipped organisations). However, it issues its annual report to analyse the world economy and make policy recommendations. The BIS president (chosen by his peers for a five-year term) also makes speeches that reveal some of its principal concerns: exchange rate stability, fiscal and monetary rectitude, prudent bank lending. The BIS has had a lot to worry about in the 1970's and 1980's.

Barter

It is an exchange of goods and services with goods and services, *e.g.* cabbages for chemicals. It is one form of counter-trade which is the generic term for many transactions where bills are paid in goods rather than money. Pure barter involves the simultaneous swapping of goods: In a playground, ten sweets for two marbles; in east-west trade, machine tools for trousers.

Below Par

Description of a share or bond whose market value is below its face value. In the bond market this happens when market interest rates are higher than they were at the time the bond was issued. It can also happen if investors change their view of the credit-worthiness of the company or government that issues the bond.

Bretton Woods

The deal that shaped the international monetary system for twenty-five years after the Second World War, and set up the International Monetary Fund (IMF) and the International Bank for Reconstruction and Development is known as the World Bank. In 1994, officials from forty-five non-communist nations met at Bretton Woods in New Hampshire, USA, and agreed on a system of international liquidity and exchange rate management, to be administered by the IMF. This was the first time that a formal world agreement had laid down rules for the international monetary system.

Under Bretton Woods, exchange rates of IMF members were fixed in terms of gold, or the dollar; but only the dollar was actually convertible into gold, at a fixed price of $ 35 an ounce. Members guaranteed to maintain their currencies' value (by buying and selling them) within one per cent either side of parity, and were required to inform the IMF of any parity changes, and needed IMF permission for changes of more than 10 per cent. The IMF rules required that changes should be made only if a country's balance of payments was in 'fundamental disequilibrium'.

For governments in payments difficulty, the Bretton Woods agreement envisaged international reserves: IMF members deposit a 'quota' of national currency (and also, until 1976, gold) with the IMF, the quota being set according to the country's importance. The IMF then uses these deposits to lend to countries in balance of payments difficulties. It could also use its holdings of *Special drawing rights (SDRs)*.

Budget

Annual rigmarole to decide how to finance public expenditure for the year ahead and how to slant fiscal policy—through changes in taxes, borrowing or expenditure. The presentation and approval of a budget is an annual exercise.

Buffer Stock

Method of stabilising commodity prices. When a commodity's price falls, buffer stock managers buy up large quantities in order to stabilise prices. Purchases are stored, and then sold off once the price is high again.

Bundes Bank

Germany's central bank, perhaps the most independent of all from government. It is housed in a dull, grey office block just outside Frankfurt, the Bunders Bank's powers and duties are vested in the federal constitution: first to safeguard the currency by fighting off inflation and second, to support the economic policy of the government.

Inter-Bank Call Market

The inter-bank call market is part of the domestic money market from where banks borrow and lend on a daily basis. The daily turnover of funds in this market is currently estimated at Rs. 8,000 crores.

All scheduled commercial banks (private sector, public sector and co-operative banks), financial institutions (term-lending institutions, insurance companies) and mutual funds can participate in this market. Non-banking finance companies, however, are not allowed to participate in this market as yet.

Participants are split into two categories. The first comprises those who can both borrow and lend in this market, and the second, those who can lend but not borrow. Only banks can do both.

Banks borrow in the call market to meet any temporary short-fall in funds on any given day. There are mainly two reasons why a bank may face such a shortfall. Banks normally lend out of the deposits that they mobilise. But there are temporary gaps, or mismatches. The call money market is used to manage these gaps.

The second reason is to meet the cash reserve ratio (CRR) which is statutory cash reserves. It must maintain with the Reserve Bank of India, to meet daily cash needs of the bank's clientale. The CRR is calculated on the basis of the bank's borrowings or the net time and demand liabilities (NDTL), broadly its deposit base, every alternate Friday. This day is also called the reporting Friday, on which the banks report their positions to the RBI. So, the CRR for the current fortnight is calculated as a per cent of the NDTL as of the last Friday.

Technically, the call money market is an overnight money market. But a bank can borrow these funds for between one day up to 14 days. Normally, funds are borrowed for one day and up to three days on weekends.

The rate of interest is calculated on daily basis; but the rate quoted in the market is an annualised one. Once the deal is struck, the funds are immediately available to the borrowing bank and is returned with interest the next day.

The funds are lent and paid back through a banker's pay order which is cleared by the special high value banker's clearing cell in the RBI.

Can the RBI Lend in the Call Market?

The RBI is the market regulator and cannot lend or borrow funds in the call market. However, as a regulator it can intervene in the market as it did when rates go through the roof. It intervenes in the market through two market intermediaries—the Securities Trading Corporation of India and the Discount Finance House of India. The STCI lends funds against the government securities that a bank holds with an offer to sell back the security (called repurchases or repos), while the DFHI lends funds that it receives from the central bank against repos of certain securities specified as eligible for them. The RBI also allows banks to rediscount proceeds of export bills of exchange.

The interest rates fluctuate in the market depending on the demand and supply of money. High rates indicate a tightness of liquidity in the financial system, while low rates indicate an easy liquidity position. In India, rates in the call market are prone to fluctuations and are unidirectional. This is due to the fact that it has a limited number of players whose needs are similar.

Effects of Cheaper Rupee

1. Indian goods with low import content generally become cheaper and thus more competitive in foreign markets. But beyond a point, this effect does not work.
2. Imports become costlier. This leads to cutbacks in imports of goods that can wait, but the import bill for essentials goes up. Domestic products with imported inputs also become costlier.
3. Domestic inflation rises because essentials like oil and fertilisers account for 40 per cent of India's imports.
4. Domestic industry enjoys enhanced protection, because imports are costlier. In the absence of competition from cheap imports, domestic prices can rise.
5. Travel overseas becomes costlier.
6. Businesses may disregard the rupee and enter into transactions in hard currencies.
7. To check erosion of wealth held in rupees (such as, in bank accounts), investors shift to gold, jewellery and land.
8. Flight of capital through hawala transactions is possible.

Hard Currency

A currency that is not likely to fall suddenly in value is a hard currency. It is called so because of its capacity to withstand economic, political or other upheaveals, such as, stock-market crash, change of government, war etc. It is easily convertible into gold or other currencies unlike soft currencies. The US dollar, the British pound sterling, the German Deutch Mark and the Japanese Yen, etc. are acknowledged as hard currencies while certain Latin American and Asian currencies are regarded as soft ones.

Eurocurrency

A currency deposited and lent outside its country of origin. The predominant Eurocurrency is the dollar (which has always accounted for more than 70 per cent of the total market), but there are also EuroDeutschmarks, Euroyen, Eurosterling and so on.

European Economic Community (EEC)

Trade, aid, agricultural and political club for western Europeans situated in Brussels, Luxembourg and Strasbourg. The EEC was founded on March 25, 1957, when six countries—France, West Germany, Belgium, Holland, Luxembourg and Italy—signed the Treaty of Rome. The EEC was a direct development from the European Coal and Steel Community founded by the above six at the Treaty of Paris in 1951, which still exists as an adjunct to the EEC. In 1973, three more members joined the club—Britain, Ireland and Denmark; in 1981 Greece joined; and in 1986 Spain and Portugal. The goods are traded in EEC countries without custom duties. The Rome treaty, and subsequent policies built upon it, have established:

A Customs Union

Inside the 12 members all quota and tariff barriers to trade have been abolished, and there is a common external tariff for imports from non-EEC members. The bulk of those enter largely unhindered by virtue of a plethora of trade deals between the EEC and its trading partners, and aid deals like the Lome Convention. Agricultural imports are, however, subject to hefty tariffs under the Common Agricultural Policy which is the EEC's only major common policy for an economic sector.

European Free Trade Association (EFTA)

Free trade club for Europe's outer circle. Set up at Stockholm in 1959, EFTA's members now are Norway, Sweden, Austria, Iceland and Switzerland. Finland has stayed out in order to appear neutral between east and west, but is, in effect, a full member. Tariffs and quotas on industrial goods between EFTA members have been phased out, and part of agricultural trade is free of duty. EFTA is not a Customs union, as it has no common external tariff, so it has elaborate rules on the flow of non-EFTA goods inside the area, and on processing for outward trade.

Originally Denmark and Britain were members, but they both deserted in 1973 to join the European Economic Community. Portugal defected when it, too, joined the EEC in 1986. EFTA has signed a series of free trade deals with the EEC that ensure virtual free trade in industrial goods between the seventeen EEC and EFTA countries.

European Monetary System (EMS)

Snake that wanted to be a prince. Born in March 1979, the EMS is a mechanism of exchange rate management between the European currencies, and a direct descendant of the so-called 'snake' system born in 1972.

The snake was hatched in response to the Smithsonian Agreement of December 1971, which allowed currencies the freedom to move by 2.25 per cent either side of their dollar parity. This meant that, against each other, European currencies could 'swing' by 9 per cent in the worst of circumstances; that is, if the Deutsch Mark was .25 per cent above its dollar parity and the French franc was .25 below, the gap between the two was .50 per cent. If they swapped positions, they would open up a .50 per cent gap the other way, making a 9 per cent swing.

The Europeans, keen to steady rates to facilitate intra EEC trade, thought this swing excessive. The Basle agreement of April 1972 set up narrower limits: the six founding members of the EEC, plus the trio soon to join (Britain, Denmark and Ireland), plus Norway, agreed to let their currencies move against each other by a maximum of only .25 per cent. This band was to be maintained within the 4.50 per cent limits against the dollar, hence the name of the 'snake in the tunnel'

Econometrics

Use of computer analysis and modelling techniques to describe in mathematical terms the relation between key economic forces such as capital, labour interest and government policies, then test the effect of changes in economic scenarios is called econometrics.

Economic Growth Rate

This is the rate of change in the gross national product (GNP) as expressed in an annual percentage. When adjusted for inflation, it is called the real economic growth rate.

Elliot Wave Theory

A pattern recognition technique that says the market follows a pattern of five years waves up and three waves down to form a cycle of eight waves and that it moves in short and long term cycles.

Factor Cost

Way of measuring output according to the costs of factors of production (land, labour and capital), rather than market prices (which are affected by indirect taxes and subsidies).

Financial Times (FT) Index

Barometer of London's stock exchange, the index is compiled and published by the daily newspaper, *The Financial Times*. The main FT measure is the 'Industrial ordinary', which gauges movements in the shares of thirty representative industrial companies. The index has a base of July, 1935 as 100. Another, more widely based index has been developed by *The Financial Times* and the stock exchange; it is known as Footsie, for FT-SE. *The Financial Times,* together with the Institute of Actuaries and the Faculty of Actuaries, calculates other indices for each main sector (*e.g.* Oil companies, gold mines) based on market capitalisation rather than crude price movements. Collectively, these sectoral indices are known as the FT actuaries indices.

Financial Market

Market for the exchange of capital and credit in the economy. Money markets concentrate on short-term debt instruments, capital markets trade in long-term debt and equity instruments. Examples of financial markets are the stock markets, commodities markets, foreign exchange markets, money markets and the debt markets.

Floating Exchange Rate

The movement of a currency's exchange rate in response to changes in demand and supply determines the rate. In floating exchange rate there is no fixed rate. This demand and supply is based on a nation's reserves of hard currency and gold, its trade balance rate of inflation, interest rates and strength of the economy.

Free and Open Market

A free market is one in which price is determined by the free, unregulated interchange of supply and demand. This is supposed to be an efficient market.

Gilt-Edged

Usually government securities and bonds, a very safe asset to hold, as the government is responsible for the payment of interests and refund. Originally, such certificates were edges with gold.

Eurobond

Bonds denominated in US dollars or other currencies are sold to investors outside the country whose currency is used. The bonds are usually issued by large underwriting groups composed of banks and issuing houses from many countries. The Eurobond market is an important source of capital for multinational companies and foreign governments, including developing nations.

Gross Domestic Product

It is best measure of economic activity in a country. Normally abbreviated to GDP, it is arrived at by adding the total value of a country's annual output of goods and services. GDP equals private consumption + investment + government expenditures + the change in stockbuilding + (exports minus imports). It is arrived by subtracting indirect taxes and adding subsidies, however, GDP can be calculated at factor cost. This measure more accurately reveals the incomes paid to factors of production. To avoid double counting of goods and services produced for intermediate use, only final production for consumption and investment is aggregated. To eliminate the effect of inflation, GDP growth is normally expressed in constant prices.

Hawala

Hawala trade is a system of bypassing the official foreign exchange channel. Operators in the trade take payment in rupee and supply dollars or other currencies against it abroad. The trade runs through a network of agents under an operator's control. Payment made in dollars abroad can also be transferred to India and the beneficiary paid in rupees. This is a method of laundering money. Foreign exchange drawing limits can also be bypassed. Hawala rates often differ from place to place within the country. Some exporters and importers resort to hawala in other ways as well such as under invoicing and over-invoicing.

Inflation

Inflation is normally a shorthand for consumer price rise expressed as an annual rate, but can apply to other prices, for example, wholesale prices, wages, etc. Rises in consumer prices steadily erode the purchasing power of a given currency unit. Inflation would matter little if it was smooth, uniform, and all incomes were adjusted perfectly in line. But it does not work like that. Economists differ in their analysis of the causes of inflation, and therefore in their prescribed cures. Monetarism holds that inflation can be reduced only by slowing down the growth of the money supply. In the words of Milton Friedman, "inflation is always and everywhere a monetary phenomenon." Many Keynesians tend to believe that inflationary pressures can exist independently of monetary conditions, to run a modern economy at low inflation and low unemployment, they say, governments need an income policy.

International Monetary Fund (IMF)

Supervisor and safety net for the International Monetary System. The Fund was set up at Bretton Woods, along with its sister institutions just across the road in Washington DC, the World Bank, to supervise the fixed exchange rate system. IMF has been more closely involved with members' economic as well as exchange rate policies, making loans while trying to enforce adjustment for payments problems. In 1967, it devised the *special drawing rights* which aimed to relieve the dollar of its reserve currency functions. In the 1970s and 1980s it has been heavily involved with the problems of third-world debt.

Each of the more than 140 members pay subscriptions or quotas to the IMF—partly determined by the size of their economies. Thus, the United States provides 19.9 per cent of quotas, West Germany 6 per cent, Japan 4.6 per cent and Britain 6.8 per cent. Quotas are paid 75 per cent in national currencies—so the IMF's coffers are stuffed with useless pesos and gourdes—and 25 per cent in foreign currencies (formerly gold, now dollars and SDRs). This means that only about half of the quota money can actually be lent.

The IMF is run by a board of executive directors, six of whom are appointed by the world's five largest economies plus Saudi Arabia (one of the fund's biggest creditors). Countries group into constituencies to elect the other fifteen. Decisions are made by the *'interim committee'* of the finance ministers which make up the board, and in an annual meeting of all members, where more bilateral and private business is done than real IMF work. The fund has a managing director (by tradition a European) and make its views known in speeches and in an annual report, which is a veritable goldmine of information.

Keynes, John Maynard (1883-1946)

English economist, he studied under Marshall at Cambridge but went on to reject large chunks of Neo-classical Economics. His best-known work was the *General Theory of Employment, Interest and Money,* published in 1936 in the depths of the Great Depression. A complicated, sometimes obtuse book, its central message was clear: economies could be in equilibrium at less than full employment, so it was for governments, through their taxing and spending policies, to ensure enough effective demand to produce full employment.

Keynes therefore switched the emphasis of policy away from Microeconomics and on to Macroeconomics, where it remained for almost forty years. His influence was enormous, governments everywhere came to accept responsibility for full employment. His critics were not silent, however, as inflation rose in the late 1960s and early 1970s, their claim that Keynesian policies were inevitably inflationary began to receive new attention. It was President Richard Nixon, who acknowledging in 1971 that 'We are all Keynesians now', simply proved the truth of one of Keynes' most famous dicta: "Practical men, who believe themselves to be quite exempt from any intellectual influences, are usually the slaves of some defunct economist. Madmen in authority, who hear voices in the air, are distilling their frenzy from some academic scribbler of a few years back!"

From 1973 on, governments ceased to be Keynesian in any literal sense. They allowed unemployment to rise without trying to expand budget deficits enough to prevent it. Keynesians—the breed remained robust, despite the practical demise of their beliefs—argued that rising unemployment proved the need for Keynesian policies. Non-Keynesians replied that the mess was caused principally by inflation, itself the product of Keynesian policies.

Letter of Credit

It is a letter issued by the bank of buyer to the seller against some guarantee that as soon as goods are supplied to the shipping company bank guarantees to make payment to seller. It is common lubricant of trade. If company A is buying widgets from company B, A's bank can issue a letter of credit as proof that B will be paid. B can then take the letter into the market (usually the commercial paper market) and swap it for cash. Also known as *bill of exchange*, or *commercial bill*.

Lombard Rate

The rate of interest which West Germany's Central bank, the Bundesbank, charges banks when it lends them money for up to three months against the collateral of certain high-quality securities is known as Lombard rate. These securities include Treasury bills, bills of exchange and fixed interest bonds issued by particular institutions (for example, the federal government). Lombard loans are made to help banks get over temporary shortages of liquidity.

Lome Convention

Successor to the Yaounde convention, it is a trade and aid agreement between the EEC and various developing countries. It was signed in Lome (capital of Togo) in 1975, and renewed in 1980 and 1985. The 66 developing countries that now belong to Lome are in Africa, the Caribbean and the Pacific (ACP), and are mainly ex-colonies of EEC countries. But note that they exclude Asia—and therefore Britain's largest ex-colonies like India, Pakistan and Bangladesh. The other EEC countries were not prepared to grant trade concessions to such large countries.

These concessions include duty-free access to the EEC market for all ACP manufactures and most tropical agricultural products (which therefore do not compete with EEC farmers). Lome also set up a scheme called Stabex, designed to compensate primary producers for part of any decline in their export earnings from the EEC caused by falling commodity prices.

London Interbank Offered Rate (LIBOR)

Applies to the interest rates in the Eurodollar market or, more simply, it is the rate top-flight banks charge each other for cash. It is most widely used in setting the terms for a loan where the interest rate will vary. The borrower agrees to pay a margin (known as the 'spread') above LIBOR—usually between half and two percentage points. The loan agreement will stipulate which LIBOR rate is to be used, for example, three-months or (more usually) six-months. Spreads over LIBOR are a good guide to how banks view different debtor countries.

Macroeconomics

The big picture, in contrast to Micro-economics which deals with the behaviour of individual markets, households and firms. Macro issues usually involve government fiscal policy and monetary control, and focus on aggregates like rate of economic growth, the level of employment, the balance of payments, inflation and so on. However, as many economists have pointed out, such aggregates grow from micro roots : a proper understanding of unemployment and inflation requires studying labour markets as well as monetary and fiscal policies.

Marshall Plan

Named after America's secretary of state, General George Marshall, who proposed giving aid to Western Europe after the Second World War to help its industries recover. A total equal to 1 per cent of American GNP (about $ 55 billion in 1981 dollars) was given between 1948 and 1952, the great bulk of it by the United States and some by Canada.

Marx, Karl (1818-1883)

German economist, sociologist and super star. Claimed and blamed as the inspiration of all kinds of things he probably never thought of, his two best-known works were the *Communist Manifesto* (1848, jointly with Friedrich Engels) and *Das Kapital* (published in four volumes between 1867 and 1910).

Contrary to popular belief, Marx was not wholly against capitalism. It was rescuing millions from 'the idiocy of rural life', he argued; and had an impressive dynamic. It was doomed, nonetheless. It would founder, Marx thought, through a shortage of demand; would concentrate economic power and wealth in ever fewer hands; and would produce a larger and ever-more-miserable proletariat. It would be replaced by the 'dictatorship of the proletariat', leading eventually to a 'withering away' of the state.

Microeconomics

The study of economics at the level of the individual household or firm, in contrast to macroeconomics. Price theory has a central role in microeconomics: how prices emerge and change, and how people respond to them. This brings in issues such as competition and availability of information, both important elements in micro behaviour. The formal distinction between micro and macroeconomics, though embodied in most textbooks, is often less than helpful. Since the early 1970s economists have renewed attempts to fuse the two, recognising that certain key macroeconomic questions like inflation and unemployment have their roots in the way prices are fixed and labour markets operate.

Mill, John Stuart

English economist and philosopher (1806-73). He is best known among economists for his *Principles of Political Economy* (1848). Modern-day political liberals and classical economists still regard the book—essentially a textbook of classical economic thought that updated Adam Smith's Wealth of Nations, rather than introducing startlingly new concepts—as an exemplary statement of their faith. Mill's upbringing was decidedly unusual, though he learned Greek at three, Latin at eight, and algebra, geometry and differential calculus by the time he was twelve.

Organization for Economic Co-operation and Development (OECD)

The capitalist world's club, the OECD has twenty four member countries and a secretariat based in Paris. Its origin go back to the Marshall plan, when the organisation for European Economic Co-operation (OEEC) was set up to organise Europe's recovery. In 1961, the OEEC became the OECD, the principal forum for countries to discuss economic issues of mutual interest.

Sceptics believe that the OECD is little more than a talking shop and a massive collector of statistics. Others point to more concrete achievements, such as, the gentleman's agreement on export credits, the co-ordination of rich-country views in north-south negotiations, and fruitful work on particular industries like shipbuilding and steel, where capacity in OECD countries clearly needed to be cut. The OECD's publications are also valuable, the annual economic surveys on each member country and the biannual Economic Outlook being particularly useful.

The OECD's twenty-four members are: Australia, Austria, Belgium, Canada, Denmark, Finland, France, West Germany, Greece, Iceland, Ireland, Italy, Japan, Luxemburg, the Netherlands, New Zealand, Norway, Portugal, Spain, Sweden, Switzerland, Turkey, the United Kingdom and the United States. In addition, Yugoslavia, communism's maverick, has a special status halfway between member and observer. The secretary-general of the OECD is by tradition a European.

Organisation of Petroleum Exporting Countries (OPEC)

OPEC became a household term in 1973-74, after oil prices were quadrupled within the space of a few weeks. It was established in 1960 to try to co-ordinate production among the main oil exporters. Its success as a cartel is hotly disputed; some economists argue that market pressures were leading to a sharp rise in oil prices anyway, and OPEC merely capitalized on them. Certainly OPEC later had difficulty in maintaining the unity it achieved in 1974.

By 1980, it was obvious that OPEC's cohesion depended on what Saudi Arabia did. It needs to produce about 5 million barrels of oil a day for its own foreign exchange requirements, but is capable of producing about 11 million b/d. This margin gives it enormous power to decide how much OPEC as a group will produce, and therefore the prices at which oil will sell. Saudi Arabia has generally used this power to moderate the ambitions of the 'OPEC hawks', such as, Algeria and Venezuela.

Not all oil exporters belong to OPEC (Britain and Mexico being two obvious exceptions), and the world's largest oil producer, the Soviet Union, is not a member either. These outsiders are one reason why OPEC's importance has diminished. In 1974, 53 per cent of all the world's oil came from OPEC members; by 1981, their share was down to 40 per cent; by 1986, it had fallen still further to around 30 per cent. Current OPEC members are Saudi Arabia, Iran, Iraq, Kuwait, UAE, Qatar, Venezuela, Nigeria, Libya, Indonesia, Algeria, Gabon and Ecuador.

Recession

It refers to a period of slow or no economic growth or of contraction. Has two more precise meanings :

Any period where GDP growth is below the assumed underlying growth in the economy's productive potential. Since that potential is, in the short term, assumed to be closely related to the availability of labour, rising unemployment is a fairly good indicator of recession (though note that since changes in unemployment lag changes in output, an economy can be recovering from recession—growing faster than its trend rate of growth.

Smith, Adam (1723-90)

Father of modern economics, his book '*Inquiry into the Nature and Causes of the Wealth of Nations*' (1776) is still regarded as a bible of classical economics. He emphasized the importance of specialization (which he called the division of labour), Techincal progress and capital investment as the main motors of economic growth. Above all, he believed in the invisible hand—the idea that free markets would ensure that the pursuit of self-interest produced benefits for all.

Special Drawing Rights (SDRs)

The nearest thing to 'world money', though of a specialised and somewhat arcane kind. SDRs were conceived in 1967 at the annual meeting of the International Monetary Fund held in Rio de Janeiro. They were introduced in 1970, as an international reserve (currency) asset intended partially to replace gold and national currencies in settling international transactions. The SDR would, it was thought, have the virtues of stability (it was first fixed in terms of gold, then of a basket of currencies) and of taking the reserve burden off the dollar's increasingly wobbly shoulders. The IMF uses SDRs for all its book-keeping purposes.

It also issues SDRs periodically to all its member countries, as a way of boosting international liquidity.

Treasury Bills

Short-term paper issued by governments in many countries. They typically carry a three-month maturity and a fixed rate of interest. They are invaluable for meeting the residual financing needs of governments during periods when revenues and receipts may be lower than expenditure. But excessive reliance on them creates problems for management. Treasury bills usually qualify as reserve assets for banks on which they can expand their lending.

United Nations Conference on Trade and Development (UNCTAD)

It began life as a conference in 1964, and promptly became a permanent agency of the UN General Assembly. It holds periodic conferences when rich and poor countries discuss everything from commodity trade to shipping and debt. The most productive of these was the 1968 conference, which resulted in the generalised system of preferences, a scheme of preferentially low tariffs for poor countries. Between these formal sessions UNCTAD organises numerous working groups; its secretariat, based in Geneva, is generally regarded as a spokesman for the developing world.

United Nations Development Programme (UNDP)

Head-quartered in New York, and formed in 1965 through the marriage of the UN Expanded Programme of Technical Assistance and the UN Special Fund. UNDP is principally concerned with technical assistance on a wide variety of projects in the developing world. Its budget ($ 670 million in 1980) comes largely from voluntary contributions from UN member governments.

United Nations Industrial Development Organisation (UNIDO)

It was established in 1967 and is based in Vienna. Its purpose is to promote industralisation in the developing world, largely through project evaluation and advice on industrial strategy. It is committed to the so-called Lima Declaration of 1975, which aims at the developing countries having a 25 per cent share of world industrial production by the end of the century.

3

History of Stock Exchanges

The stock market provides a market place for the purchase and sale of securities. The earliest records of security dealings in India are meagre and obscure. The East India Company was the dominant institution and business in its loan securities used to be transacted towards the close of the 18th Century.

By 1830's, there was a perceptible increase in the volume of business, not only in loans but also in corporate stocks and shares. In Bombay, business passed in the shares of banks like The Commercial Bank, The Chartered Mercantile Bank, The Chartered Bank, The Oriental Bank and last the Old Bank of Bombay. Among other prominent shares were those of cotton presses.

In Calcutta, the English man reported in 1836 the quotations of 4 per cent, 5 per cent and 6 per cent loans of the East India Company as well as of the shares of the Bank of Bengal for which there were buyers at Rs. 5,000 premium and sellers at a premium of Rs. 7,500.

The trading list was broader in 1839 and Calcutta newspapers then gave quotations of banks like the Union Bank and the Agra Bank and business ventures like the Bengal Bonded Warehouse, the Docking Company and the Steam Tug Company. Brokers then were not numerous community and in Bombay between 1840 and 1850, there were half a dozen brokers recognised by the banks and merchants.

In 1850, the Companies Act, introducing limited liability was enacted and with it commenced the era of modern joint stock enterprises in India.

Premchand Roychand

From 1850 to 1865, the history of brokers and their rise to power in Bombay is the history of Premchand Roychand. The 1850's witnessed a rapid development of commercial enterprises. The extension of railways and introduction of Telegraphs and the gradual improvement in the system of communications promoted internal trade and commerce. The demand for European manufactures increased in India. It was accompanied by the growth of a corresponding demand in Europe for our exports. Stockbrokers shared in this general progress. The *hundi* business was most prosperous and so was that of brokerage.

Brokerage business attracted many men into the field and by 1860 the number of brokers increased to 60. Their acknowledged leader was the legendary Premchand Roychand who had entered the trade in 1850. He was the first broker who could speak and write English. Within six or seven years, he nearly monopolised the broking business in shares, stocks, bullion and partly exchange and gathered all the strings in his hands. Not only shares but also all the gilt-edged securities of those days gave him a splendid opportunity for the display of brilliant strategy which crowned him with the title of Napoleon of France and he was acclaimed as much by myriads of his countrymen.

Although, Premchand Roychand remained a broker all his life, in the 1860's he directed his commercial genius to other pursuits. He held captive the imagination of Indians and Europeans alike and all the enterprises were either promoted by him or promoted through his goodwill and help. He floated banks and financial institutions by the dozen.

Premchand Roychand wielded the spectre of kings. The Old Bank of Bombay and the Asiatic Bank belonged to him. The story of the boom that followed his activities was indeed a marvellous history more fascinating in its accidents than many a tale of Arabian Nights. He was the master mind in finance which wrought those marvellous miracles on the stock exchange.

American Civil War and the Boom

In 1860-61, the American Civil War broke out and totally stopped the supply of cotton from the United States to

Europe. The resulting cotton famine led to the large and unlimited demand on India. India really meant the Bombay Presidency where the largest stocks were available. In four years, exports fully doubled themselves from 5,66,000 bales to 11,18,000 bales.

As the civil war progressed, the price of cotton kept rising till it reached 27 d. per pound against 3 d. to 5 d. quoted before 1863. The large exports of cotton were paid for in bullion which poured into Bombay from Liverpool in the shape of silver and gold. The total import of bullion amounted to Rs. 85 crores between 1861-62 and 1864-65. Of this, Bombay alone absorbed Rs. 52 crores, giving an average of Rs. 13 crores per annum.

The import of bullion was in addition to the wealth of the city which served as fresh capital for a number of new ventures. As observed by the Bank of Bombay Commission in its report:

> "The great and sudden wealth produced by the price of cotton shortly after the commencement of the American war, coupled with the want of legitimate means of investment, was at this time producing its natural result in the development of excessive speculation. . . From this period everyone in Bombay appears to have become wild with the spirit of speculation. Companies were started for every imaginable purpose—banks and financial associations, land reclamation, trading, cotton cleaning, pressing and spinning, hotel companies, shopping and steamer companies and companies for making bricks and tiles."

Between 1863-65, the capital drawn into these new ventures was nearly Rs. 30 crores and the premia they fetched in the market amounted to nearly Rs. 38 crores. More than 125 concerns were involved and in quite a few cases, the premia exceeded the paid-up capital.

The first vital spark of speculation which burst out into a huge conflagration was kindled by the Asiatic Banking Corporation, originally named the Bombay Joint Stock Bank. It was established in 1863 with a capital of Rs. 50 lakhs which was doubled within a year when a charter was obtained. Its shares were rigged up to a premium of 65 per cent in a few months.

It was also in 1863 that the charter of the Old Bank of Bombay was amended and its capital doubled from Rs. 52 lakhs to Rs. 104 lakhs. At the same time, the ban on the bank prohibiting it from making advances on personal security was removed and permission to advance on government securities was enlarged to cover securities of "other public companies in India". This new freedom was fully exploited. Premchand Roychand dominated the bank and under his influence, the bank advanced on a variety of supposedly substantial securities with highly fictitious value. The reckless lending policy of the Bank of Bombay was in large measure imitated by others. This was considerably responsible for the speculation that followed.

From 1861 to the beginning of 1865, there was nothing, however wild that was floated whose shares did not command a premium. The Back Bay Reclamation share with Rs. 5,000 paid-up was at Rs. 50,000 premium, the Port Canning share with Rs. 1,000, paid-up at Rs. 11,000 premium, while the Mazagaon Land share was at Rs. 9,000 premium and the Elphinstone Land share at more than 500 per cent premium.

Some of the banks and financial associations reached a premium of 50 per cent to 100 per cent without being tested by returns. The Asiatic Bank share of Rs. 200 was quoted at Rs. 400 in August 1864 and the Bank of Bombay share with Rs. 500 paid-up reached a maximum price of Rs. 2,850.

It was said that "man and woman, master and servant, employer and employee, banker and merchant, trader and artisan, rich and poor, of all races and creed, officials in high position included", were deeply busy from day-to-day in the art of commuting bits of paper, variously called 'allotments', 'scrips' and 'shares' into gold and silver. The madness which seized the people was indescribable. The people only woke up when the end of the American Civil War came. Then all rushed to sell their securities but there were no buyers and the entire wealth received during the civil war was represented by a huge mass of unsaleable paper.

Depression of 1865

The fatal day came on July 1, 1865 when hundreds of time bargains matured which no one was in a position to fulfil. A disastrous slump followed and it completely overwhelmed the city. Bank of Bombay share which had previously touched Rs. 2,850 could only be sold at Rs. 87 and the Back Bay Reclamation share at not more than Rs. 1,750 against a peak price of Rs. 50,000 premium, while the share of the Solid Elphinstone Company could only be sold at Rs. 450.

Like the South Sea Bubble and the Tulip Mania of the 18th century in Europe, the share mania of 1861-65 caused widespread desolation. Premchand Roychand and his broker friends were "anthematifed". A large number of companies failed and there were few left solvent in Bombay. A special legislation was enacted in 1865 to deal with the company's failures. The liquidation went on till 1872.

The depression was long and severe, but the share mania had certain lasting effects. The expansion of liquid capital and the establishment of a regular market in securities were its direct results and they helped to make Bombay what it is today—the chief centre of the money and the capital market of India.

Bombay Stock Exchange

During the share mania of 1861-65, the number of brokers greatly increased and came to wield great influence, authority and wealth. Between 1840 and 1850, only half a dozen brokers had sufficed for the limited business that then existed and their meeting place was under the widespreading banyan trees in front of the Town Hall at the Cotton Green where the Elphinstone or Horniman Circle is now situated. Brokers continued to meet there till 1855 by which time their number had increased to 40.

By 1860, the number of brokers was 60 and during the exciting period of the American civil war, their number increased to 250. Brokers were a privileged class, created as much noise as they pleased and obstructed without let or hindrance the streets, the steps and the lower premises of banks. Bank managers went to their rooms through a serried rank of brokers, bowing to them right and left. The police also saluted them.

The end of the American civil war brought disillusionment and many failures. The brokers decreased in number and prosperity. Bank managers, all of a sudden, discovered that the brokers were a nuisance to their customers and ordered that brokers be cleared from their steps. The brokers had to shift from place to place till 1874 when they went to a street, now called the *Dalal Street*.

The Bombay Stock Exchange was founded in 1875, the entrance fee for new members was Re. 1. There were 318 members on the list. The number of members increased to 333 in 1896, 362 in 1916 and 478 in 1920. The entrance fee was raised to Rs. 500 in 1877, Rs. 1,000 in 1896, Rs. 2,500 in 1916 and Rs. 48,000 in 1920.

The organisation of the Bombay Stock Exchange coincided with the recovery from the 7-year depression following share mania of 1861-65. After 1872, the brokers promoted only those enterprises which were useful and remunerative, especially mills, presses and mining companies.

The Bombay Stock Exchange played an important part in the new developments. The object of forming an association with fixed rules for conduct and settlement of business was to facilitate the negotiations of the sale and purchase of joint stock securities promoted throughout the Presidency of Bombay. In this, the association entirely succeeded. Outside the Presidency, no securities would be negotiated, purchased or sold.

In those days, it was very difficult to float a public limited company and secure large amounts of capital subscribed. It goes to the credit of the brokers that they always tried their best to popularise the new issue to enable the companies to secure the necessary capital. The stock exchange channelled the flow of investment into stocks, shares and gilt-edged securities and materially helped government, trade and industry.

As the exchange grew in size, so did its accommodation. The premises taken in 1874 in Dalal Street on a rent of Rs. 130 per month which is now known as the Stock Exchange old building, situated at Dalal Street, and was acquired for Rs. 97,000 in 1895.

Ahmedabad Stock Exchange—1920

The cotton textile industry which established the primacy of Bombay also contributed to the development of Ahmedabad as the next important city in the Bombay Presidency. After 1880, a number of textile mills were set up in Ahmedabad and it rapidly forged ahead. Soon the need arose for trading in the shares of those units which were incorporated as joint stock companies. The businessmen of Ahmedabad had inherited a tradition for dealing in stocks and shares. Many of them had actively participated in the share mania of 1861-65 in Bombay. In fact, a number of Bombay brokers hailed from Ahmedabad. As new cotton textile mills were floated, Ahmedabad brokers canvassed subscriptions for the capital issues of these companies. The volume of business steadily grew till 1894, the brokers formed themselves into an association under the name and style of "The Ahmedabad Share and Stock Broker's Association".

The exchange was organised as a voluntary non-profit-making association on the same lines as the Bombay Stock Exchange. The Ahmedabad market concentrated its business in the shares of local textile mills and of the managing agency houses, controlling these companies.

After the First World War, a substantial increase in its trading volume led the exchange to have a building in the Manek chowk area where the members used to congregate and trade under the open sky.

Beginning of the Swadeshi Movement

The beginning of the 20th century saw the birth of the swadeshi movement. The institution of the Indian Industrial Conference in 1905 in association with the Indian National Congress was the first definite sign of an alliance between economic and political discontent. The swadeshi movement let loose a great wave of industrial enthusiasm in the country and an important stage in industrial advance under Indian enterprise was reached with the inauguration of the Tata Iron and Steel Co. Ltd. in 1907. These developments were portents of the industrial progress to come and of the part to be played by the Stock exchanges.

Calcutta Stock Exchange

The Stock exchanges at Bombay and Ahmedabad were well set up as properly organised associations at the commencement of the 20th century, but the Calcutta Stock Exchange was not so consolidated.

At that time, the only large organised industries on a stable footing were the cotton mill industry of western India, the jute industry in Bengal and coal and mining industry in Bihar, Orissa and Bengal. What the cotton industry was to Bombay in the West, the jute industry was to Calcutta in the East.

The jute mills were beginning to spring up on the banks of the Hooghly when Bombay was in the grip of the share mania during 1861-65. These were also boom years in Calcutta. In 1964 there were 91 joint stock companies in which business was being done. Of these the largest group was tea, consisting of 38 companies. The coal section was represented by Bengal, Birbhum, East Indian, Equitable and another company. Jute Mills attained an important place in the trading list. In the 1870's there was a sharp boom in jute shares.

The boom in jute shares was followed by a boom in tea shares in the 1880's and 1890's. As the century drew to a close, the 4 per cent government paper (converted into 3.5 per cent government paper in 1901) was an important market leader in Calcutta and the major industrial groups were teas, jute and coal.

After a few years there was a coal boom in Calcutta and between 1904 and 1908, coal shares staged a remarkable rise. Burrakur which was quoted at Rs. 85 in 1902 jumped upto Rs. 540 in 1908, Bengal Nagpur from Rs. 22 to Rs. 104, Raneegunge from Rs. 11 to Rs. 43. Dazzled by price rise, many persons who had never dealt in shares were attracted to stock exchange as moths to a candle. Hectic buying raised prices to the roof. At last, the boom broke in 1908 and a severe depression followed.

The crisis that followed the boom provoked differences and disputes among brokers and ultimately led to communal riot in May 1908. It was then realised that an organised body was necessary for the mutual protection and safety of the brokers. Consequently, brokers formed an association on June 15, 1908 known as "The Calcutta Stock Exchange Association".

When the Calcutta Stock Exchange Association was constituted, the number of founder members was about 150. The place where it is housed now is known as the Lyons Range. The Calcutta Stock Exchange had to face problems.

Shortly after its formation in 1908, the severe trade depression that followed on the heels of the coal boom, took a heavy toll. Many stockbrokers sustained heavy losses and abandoned the trade while some others defaulted and were expelled. Financial difficulties were so acute that in the early part of 1910, the association seriously considered whether it should not wind up its affairs.

These difficulties were, however, surmounted because it was recognised that the Calcutta Stock Exchange performed a most useful function as a principal market in Bengal and Eastern India for stocks, shares and securities.

First World War Boom

On the eve of the First World War the stock market in India consisted of three stock exchanges at Bombay, Calcutta and Ahmedabad. As hostilities intensified, Europe ceased to produce any manufactured article except those required for the prosecution of the war. The import of manufactures into India stopped and a boom ensued in all industrial enterprises.

Mills, factories and workshops worked round-the-clock, fabulous profits were earned and large dividends were declared. Cotton and jute textiles, steel, sugar, paper and flour mills and all companies generally enjoyed phenomenal prosperity. Wealth accumulated and the volume of money increased. The stock exchanges became the centre of attraction for all.

The roaring trade in stocks and shares during the war and post-war boom led to the formation of rival stock exchanges in Bombay and Ahmedabad. A new limited company was formed and incorporated in Bombay under the name of the Bombay Stock Exchange Ltd. in December 1917 and an un-incorporated body called the Gujarat Share and Stock Exchange was established in Ahmedabad in 1920.

The Bombay Stock Exchange Ltd. had its own managing committee, a number of well-known industrialists and businessmen like Sri Purshothamdas, Thakurdas, Sir Chunilal V. Mehta, Sir Ibrahim Rahimtoolla, Mr. Rameshwardas Birla and others. These were men with high reputation but were not conversant with the working of the stock exchanges. Ultimately, these stock exchanges had to close down.

Foundation of the Madras Stock Exchange

The war and post-war boom was followed by a world depression in 1930's. The improvement in business conditions and in stock market activity in 1935 was marked by growing public interest in stocks, shares and securities. In South India, there was a rapid increase in the number of textile mills and many new plantation companies were floated. To cater to this expanding trade in plantation and mill shares, a stock exchange was organised in Madras on September 4, 1937. When the Madras Stock Exchange was established it had five members and 84 companies.

The Second World War

The Second World War touched off a sharp boom which was followed by a slump. The situation changed radically in 1943 when India was fully mobilised as a supply base. Mills, factories and workshops were running day and night. Prosperity was rapidly increasing, inflationary finance expanded, money became cheaper and paper wealth multiplied. This war-time boom brought unprecedented prosperity to the stock exchanges. On account of restrictive controls on cotton, bullion, seeds and other commodities, those dealing in them found in the stock market the only outlet for their activities. They were anxious to join the trade and their number swelled. Many new associations were formed for the purpose of organising stock exchanges in all parts of the country.

Brokers Rise

In Ahmedabad where the Ahmedabad Share and Stock Brokers Association recognised by the government already existed, as many as four new stock exchanges were set up. In Calcutta, over and above the existing Calcutta Stock Exchange Association Ltd., the Bengal Share and Stock Exchange Association Ltd., a third Exchange called the Stock Exchange Association of Bengal Ltd. was organised.

In Delhi, two stock exchanges, the Delhi Stock and Share Broker's Association Ltd. and The Delhi Stocks and Shares Exchange Ltd. were floated. Later on June 25, 1947, they were amalgamated into Delhi Stock Exchange Association Ltd.

Registration and Recognition of Stock Exchanges

The Bangalore Stock Exchange was registered in 1957 and was recognised in 1963. Fourteen more stock exchanges were recognised, the Cochin Stock Exchange Ltd. in 1980, the Uttar Pradesh Stock Exchange Association Ltd. (at Kanpur) and the Pune Stock Exchange Ltd. in 1982, the Ludhiana Stock Exchange Association Ltd. in 1983, the Gauhati Stock Exchange Ltd. in 1984, the Kanara Stock Exchange Ltd. (at Mangalore) in 1985, The Magadh Stock Exchange Association (at Patna) in 1986, The Jaipur Stock Exchange Ltd., the Bhubaneswar Stock Exchange Association Ltd., the Saurashtra Kutch Stock Exchange Ltd., the Over-the-Counter (OTC) Exchange of India in 1989, The Vadodara Stock Exchange Ltd. in 1990, the Coimbatore Stock Exchange Ltd. in 1991.

The OTC exchange was promoted jointly by the ICICI, UTI, SBI Capital Markets Ltd.

A stock exchange was established in Sikkim in 1985. No official recognition for this exchange has been sought under the 1956 Securities Contracts Act as the jurisdiction of this Act has not been extended to the state of Sikkim. The number of stock exchanges in the country increased from 7 in 1946 to 23 in 1994.

The stock market in India is more than a century old. At present, there are twenty-three recognised stock exchanges. They are at Ahmedabad, Bangalore, Baroda, Bhubaneswar, Bombay—Bombay (OTC), Bombay (National Stock Exchange), Calcutta, Cochin, Coimbatore, Delhi, Gauhati, Hyderabad, Indore, Jaipur, Kanpur, Ludhiana, Madras, Mangalore, Patna, Pune, Rajkot, Meerut and Gangtok.

These recognised stock exchanges operate under the rules, bye-laws and regulations approved by the government and they constitute an organised capital market for securities issued by the Central and state Governments, public bodies and joint stock companies.

4

Comparison between Bombay Stock Exchange and National Stock Exchange

The Bombay Stock Exchange is 125 years old. It is the oldest exchange in India. It has dominated the stock market like a colossus till the nineties. In March 1995, BSE began screen trading with the introduction of the BSE On-Line Trading System. Automated trading which began shakily with 818 scrips was soon extended to cover 5,000 scrips within fifty days.

Today, BSE has been overtaken by the National Stock Exchange which was set up in 1993. This is evident when one compares the turnover at the BSE with the NSE. The signs were evident as far back as 1993. The total turnover on BSE dropped from Rs. 84,536 crore in 1993-94 to Rs. 67,749 crore in 1994-95 and further to Rs. 50,664 crore in 1995-96.

Since November 1995, NSE's daily turnover has consistently overtaken that of BSE. Average daily turnover at NSE in October 1995 was Rs. 148 crore to BSE's Rs. 258 crore. But in November 1995, NSE's average daily turnover rose to Rs. 259 crore and the BSE's average daily turnover declined to Rs. 187 crore.

In July 1996, NSE's daily average turnover was Rs. 1,687 crore, more than double of BSE's Rs. 632 crore. This happened despite the fact that 2,257 more companies were listed on BSE in the past two years which should have increased volumes substantially.

Even the value of the BSE membership card has gone down. A foreign investment bank picked up the card in an auction in March 1996 for Rs. 2.61 crore. An Indian corporate picked up the card for Rs. 2.11 crore. The ruling price for BSE card has been over Rs. 3 crore. The shrinking broking income on the exchange and stiff competition from NSE are said to be the main reasons behind the lower realisation from the sale of a BSE membership card.

Brokers attribute it to sharp decline in brokerage following the introduction of the screen-based trading. Brokerages have plummeted to just about half a per cent for large deals from an average of 1.5 to 2 per cent of trade value due to competition from brokers on BSE and the entry of the corporate sector in the stock broking business. A prominent BSE broker said that it made sense to get out of BSE and do business only on NSE. He feels that with a Rs. 55 lakh deposit plus working capital, NSE provides a nationwide network for trading in securities.

Operational Change in BSE

BSE has taken up the challenge to outpace NSE. To achieve this, it approached the Financ Ministry to give it permission for BOLT expansion. BSE has offered the regional exchange tie up with it once the process of expansion starts. The permission has been granted in July 1997. It has been permitted to have operations in 99 centres through VSAT. This would help BSE's 4,200 active scrips to be traded nationwide.

With the introduction of BOLT, BSE has introduced series of reforms in its trading, settlement and clearance systems.

In February 1996, BSE introduced weekly settlements for the A and BI groups (450 shares carved out of the B group) which cover 90 per cent of the volume of business by shorter trading cycles in a bid to boost volumes.

The large B group, however, is still on a fortnightly cycle. BSE is assuring the capability of its clearing house. As soon as it is able to deal with the additional volumes, B group scrips would be put on a weekly trading cycle.

The settlement systems, too, has been reduced to a week to conform with the trading cycle.

In June 1996, BSE automated its auction system also for bad deliveries—online auctions are conducted within eight days of the settlement period for shares from all the three groups. Also there is one auction cycle now compared to the several earlier which was thoroughly misused by operators to boost prices. So, the incentive for the price rigging has been taken away.

On August 7, 1996, BSE became the first exchange to introduce odd-lot trading. This gives the exchange a national stature, as no other exchange including NSE, has been willing to extend this service.

BSE plans to introduce a debt market segment with the advent of big bond issues. The existing BSE members would undertake this business so that there is no extra load on the brokerage. BSE will also introduce futures trading once the Securities Contract Act is amended.

Existing systems, too, are being constantly upgraded. BSE has drawn up a blueprint for the revamp of its bad delivery and objections procedure, which will be implemented soon. Bad deliveries are the biggest concern of exchanges and investors today. Eighty per cent of the bad deliveries arise because of signature differences.

Under the new system, BSE clearing house, BOI Shareholding, has been appointed as the central agency for settlement of company objections and the exchange will also directly involve the custodians who are operating for FIS and FIIs to streamline the delivery process. Delivering members will have to rectify objections within three weeks. The exchange will also guarantee resolutions of objections which led to the bad delivery.

Besides, BSE has also addressed over 700 corporate houses asking them to redress shareholders grievances. It has also altered the listing clause, laying down fresh procedures that listed companies must adopt while dealing with signature-difference related bad deliveries.

Screen-based trading has not only improved transparency on the BSE, but has also made online surveillance possible. BSE intends to go beyond scrip surveillance to monitor price movements for which it is building database.

In recent months, BSE has introduced controls through suspension of scrips. It has also been taking, alongwith Sebi, sterner action against erring brokers, and has begun impounding auction proceeds.

Reliance Duplicate Share Issues

In August 1995, Reliance Industries Ltd., one of India's biggest private company, a petrochemical and textile giant, fought a fierce battle against the BSE over the issue of 40,000 duplicate shares. These shares were issued by RIL when the original shares had already been lodged with them for registration.

This fight brought about a sharp fall in the Reliance Scrip which touched a low of Rs. 198 from Rs. 280. The decline in the RIL share price made a dent of 500 points in the BSE 30-share index called sensex. The index dropped below 2,900. RIL enjoyed the highest weightage along with the Tata Steel in the index. Now SAIL enjoys the highest weightage.

RIL has 2.6 million shareholders. At present, its turn-over accounts for about 40 per cent of the aggregate turnover on the BSE.

Of the 40,000 duplicate shares issued by RIL, 26,650 shares were issued to the physiotherapist, Ms. Rajul Vasa, who is looking after the ailing chairman of the company, Mr. Dhirubhai Ambani. Ms. Vasa is said to have collected cash from brokers by selling the original shares and then obtained duplicates on the ground that the shares were lost.

On August 22, 1995 BSE threatened action against RIL including delisting of its shares on account of issuance of duplicate shares for a block of 26,650 shares on September 22, 1995. BSE issued a show-cause notice to RIL.

RIL explained that the matter of issuing duplicate shares has been blown out of proportion and sensationalised for ulterior motives. It said that neither the government nor Sebi nor the exchanges have laid down detailed guidelines for issuing of duplicate shares.

It contended that certain procedures have been involved in this regard in the industry and the same are being followed by all transfer agents. It claimed that the Reliance Consultancy Services (RIL, transfer agents) acted responsibly and in a bonafide manner and followed these conventional and well recognised procedures. It further contended that the concerned originals had been lodged for transfer and it never came to the notice of the section processing the request for issue of duplicate share certificates and the two events could not be linked at that time. The transfer request and duplicate certificates requests are handled by different sections.

When the BSE served notice to RIL that Ms. Vasa had alledgedly obtained duplicate shares, Reliance took legal advice and acting in good faith invoked the idemnity bond given by her and paid Rs. 1.06 crore to BSE.

Followed by the controversy of 40,000 duplicate shares, the Unit Trust of India stated that a lot of 8.70 lakh shares purchased in December 1991 from RIL were replaced by duplicate one's.

BSE expressed dissatisfaction with RIL explanation and suspended trading of its scrips from November 14, 1995 to November 17.

Later, it was found that RIL had switched 46.9 lakh original shares to duplicate one's, majority of which belonged to UTI.

On December 19, 1995, the Finance Ministry decided to conduct a joint probe by the Sebi and the Department of Company Affairs (DCA) into the transactions of RIL relating to issue of duplicate shares by RIL and the switching of RIL shares bought by UTI at the time of transfer by Reliance Consultancy Services Limited (RCS).

On July 5, 1996, Sebi in its final report recommended that the originals of the 46.9 lakh switched shares should be returned to UTI, Canfina and Canara Bank. It suggested that the licence of Reliance Consultancy Services (RCS) to function as a registrar and share transfer agent should be cancelled.

Sebi also recommended that the Department of Company Affairs should take necessary action against RIL and RCS for violations of the Companies Act.

Reacting to the Sebi report, RIL refused to admit guilt in the share switch and duplicate share case. RIL in a letter to the Registrar of Companies (ROC) stated that it was ready to pay any fine imposed on it. ROC has forwarded this offer to the Company Law Board.

Going by the fines stated in the show-cause notices dated June 7, sent to the company, RIL, if found guilty, would have to pay Rs. 1.25 crores, which industry observers say, is a small sum for the burial of the controversy.

Risk management, too, has assumed greater importance at BSE. For one, the exchange took a comprehensive, integrated insurance policy covering the exchange, the clearing house and all the members. It is also setting up a corpus of about Rs. 150 crores to guarantee all trades. In future, any defaulting member business will be fulfilled by the exchange. The corpus fund is likely to be administered by the exchange.

The margin system has also been harmonised. BSE has planned a contingency fund, which will provide a line of credit to anyone in temporary distress. Both the contingency fund and the trade guarantee corpus will ensure that the movement of scrips and payments at the exchange would not be disrupted, thus increasing investors confidence.

Despite such exhaustive reforms, the problems remain. For instance, although carry-forward or a revised *badla* was re-introduced in 32 A-group scrips on BSE last year, it has not succeeded both in terms of volume and the number of participants. The carry-forward volumes in the old system were between Rs. 300 crore and Rs. 400 crore per settlement (then 15 days) in 1992. Today, the carry-forward volume per settlement (weekly) is a mere Rs. 50 crore.

Also carry-forward in its earlier form was applicable to larger A group of around 60 odd scrips while the present A group comprises just 32 scrips. Under the earlier system, since there was no demarcation, all brokers carried forward trade. Today, with brokers having to specify cash and carry-forward position, less than 150 brokers are said to be participating in carry-forward. Carry-forward has not taken off because of stringent requirements.

The limits, too, are unworkable since brokers already have to comply with market-to-market margins and capital adequacy requirements.

Brokers are also struggling against the shift in business from retail or individual investors to institutions. In terms of delivery, institutional trade has gone up from around 30 per cent of total deliveries to over 60 per cent in the last three years (1993-96). This shift in business has hit brokers at BSE quite badly. Volumes have fallen, leading to a fall in brokerage, both due to the loss of outstation deals and the lower rates on the screen-based system.

Foreign brokers have been the main beneficiaries of liberalisation since FIIs trade through them. They have huge amounts of capital and credit lines with banks and so are able to trade comfortably, while the Indian broker has to rely on his own resources and does not have an access to finance.

National Stock Exchange

The National Stock Exchange started its operations on November 3, 1994. NSE was set up by 16 financial institutions and banks of the country who are also important participants in both the debt and equity markets. NSE was set up to bring transparency in the capital market operations.

NSE currently operates from 67 centres, spread over 126 cities. Thirty one of these centres are non-exchange points. NSE will spread its network to 200 centres by the end of 1997.

The trading system at the NSE, known as NEAT (National Exchange for Automated Trading) is fully automated screen-based trading system which enables members from across the country to trade simultaneously with enormous ease and efficiency. The trading members on the capital market segment are connected via satellite network, owned, operated and managed by NSE.

NSE is an All-India exchange that connects brokers all over the country through satellite. Brokers sit in front of their screens and feed their bids and offers on PC and get confirmations. Besides being transparent, it is very fast and investor-friendly.

The payment and delivery systems are fast and efficient. Investors do not have to wait till doomsday to get their payment. Finally the market access for them has improved substantially through NSE system.

To illustrate the point, under the old system if an investor in Delhi wished to trade in Bajaj Auto or Asian Paints, he ended up paying double brokerage to brokers in Delhi and Bombay exchanges as these top class shares are not listed in Delhi. This tended to place investors outside Bombay at a great disadvantage in terms of speed, rates and commission. With the NSE, such problems do not exist. More than 95 per cent of the active shares are on the NSE, and one can deal in all of them sitting in one's city.

Apart from systems improvement, by enrolling a large number of brokers and giving them an all-India reach, NSE has totally changed the supply-demand scenario. There are large number of brokers who have paid huge amounts and taken NSE membership—something unheard of two years ago.

NSE caught increasing media attention in November 1995. Reliance threatened to delist its shares from the Bombay Stock Exchange and shift over to NSE. However, the whole episode ended after BSE made a request to Reliance Industries not to delist its shares from the BSE in the larger interest of the investors.

Commenting on this, market experts said though Reliance had taken its decision back, the atmosphere during the period changed the sentiment in the capital market for quite sometime and it has reflected in the increased volume on the National Stock Exchange.

NSE was also in the news when it took the decision to curtail its holidays in a year. There was a mixed reaction to this decision among the brokers who are working at both the exchanges. NSE shortened the Christmas holidays by availing only a day's holiday compared to nine days holiday at the BSE.

In a short span of two years, the proactive NSE has overtaken the 120 year-old Bombay Stock Exchange. At the end of July 1996, average daily turnover at the NSE was Rs. 1659.21 crores compared with BSE's Rs. 622.8 crores. Exactly a year ago, NSE's daily turnover stood at Rs. 99 crores against BSE's Rs. 241.80 crores.

It has also been observed that the foreign institutional investors (FIIS) business is gravitating towards NSE. At the end of 1995, NSE accounted for 17 per cent of FII purchases from the secondary market with BSE at 77 per cent. Today, Sebi sources claim, NSE's share has almost doubled while BSE's is on the decline.

The trading and settlement period have a fixed schedule on NSE. Trading period commences on Wednesday and ends on the following Tuesday. Owing to weekly trading and settlement periods, the element of speculation is less and hence it is truly a cash market.

NSE's one-week settlement cycle carries a penalty for bad or delayed deliveries. If there is a shortage, the lots are auctioned in the same week. The price differential is then debited in the same manner to the defaulting broker. If it is a bad delivery, it is rectified within 48 hours and if there is a signature difference, it is rectified within 21 days.

How is this an improvement on the BSE system? BSE followed a fortnightly settlement cycle. With no support systems, bad deliveries had always posed a problem. Often, deliveries would take as long as two months. A signature difference took in some cases more than six months to be rectified. Today, BSE has cut its settlement period to a week, but bad deliveries continue to plague the system.

For all the plaudits, NSE has its share of critics, and chief among them is the BSE President, Mr. M.G. Damani. He says that nepotism is aglore in the NSE and it is of the worst kind. A common allegation is that Sebi has double standards while dealing with NSE and BSE. While it has allowed NSE to expand, it has put BSE on the leash.

Although Sebi has abolished *badla* system on BSE, brokers claim speculation largely drives trading at NSE. According to Mr. U.R. Bhatt, Chief Investment Officer of Jardine Fleming, with the scrapping of the *badla* system, NSE is the best alternative for daily cup of speculation. It has become a sort of a Casino.

Even though NSE volumes are much higher (25 per cent more than BSE in the last six months) than that of BSE, actual deliveries account for only 10 to 12 per cent of total trade. Deliveries on BSE hover between 15 to 17 per cent.

Only a handful of big scrips account for higher volumes on NSE. Ninety per cent of the traded volumes come from scrips, namely; Reliance, State Bank of India, Tisco and ACC.

5

Over the Counter Exchange of India (OTCEI)

The prevailing stock markets structure has been in such a bad state that the need for a better, fully automated and transparent exchange was felt.

The equity culture in our country has gradually spread far and wide, even to rural areas, towns and cities where no stock exchange exists and where small investors abound. Investors have been facing many problems. Companies who wanted to enlist their shares did not have alternative other than listing on the existing stock exchanges. Certain listing guidelines also prevented small and medium-sized companies from getting listed on the stock exchanges.

Investors Problems

The Indian investor has been an underdog in most deals on the stock markets, whether it be the primary market or the secondary market. The problems have been more pronounced when stock markets have been volatile. It is only recently that with the advent of Sebi that a more visible effort is being made to protect investors interests. Some of the most common problems faced by investors are:

1. Access

The foremost problem for an investor has been to have an access to a stock exchange and more importantly, to a stock broker. For most investors a stock exchange may not be available or even if it is available, it might not be easily accessible.

Krishan Kumar is a Bombay-based company executive who invests part of his savings in the stock market. He sometimes applies in public issues as well as buys shares directly from the market. Krishan was transferred by his company to Vadodra. When he wanted to sell some of his shares, he would not easily find a stock broker. When he did locate, the broker refused to deal with a stranger. When he found a willing broker through a friend, the broker informed him that the shares he wanted to sell were not listed on the Baroda Stock Exchange and Krishan would have to sell it in Bombay only.

2. Liquidity

The vast price differential quoted by market operators, as well as the absence of regular jobbers (Market makers) in various scrips has often been felt by investors. This has often resulted in severe lack of liquidity of scrips, especially when the stock markets are in throes of disarray. During the second quarter of 1992 when the stock markets all over the country were in turmoil, the problem was so pronounced that the investors stopped considering their holdings in shares as liquid assets.

Our friend Narinder wanted some money for buying furniture in his new house. When he asked his broker to sell 500 shares of ABC Ltd., the broker could sell only 200 shares because the jobber giving quotation was not prepared to buy a larger number. The price difference between buy and sell quotes by the jobber too was almost 25 per cent. Hence, if Narinder wanted to buy shares, he could buy for Rs. 50 but if he wanted to sell the same shares, they would fetch him only Rs. 40 per share. Narinder had no option.

3. Payment and Delivery Problems

It's quite unlikely that an investor has not faced either a problem of late payment for shares sold or obtaining delivery of scrips purchased in the open market. The less fortunate among us have also had problem of running after brokers for rectifying bad delivery of shares due to difference in signature of the seller or duplicate one's. During bull phases, volumes are so high that due to infrastructural problems, investors have been known to receive payments after almost two months.

Ajit who required money urgently when he sold his shares got the sale proceeds after a month. Meanwhile, Ajit's friend Madhavan told him that XYZ Ltd. was an excellent investment buy and was sure to yield handsome appreciation. Ajit bought

200 shares of XYZ after making a provision for some funds. He got delivery after 45 days. Till then his funds lay unused.

I bought shares of Gujarat Optical and Harig Crankshaft in September, 1995 and sent them for transfer to the respective companies in November, 1995. Till March, 1996, what to talk of transfer of shares, I did not even receive any acknowledgement. This is despite the fact that I had sent them registered reminders.

I had the same experience with Harig Crankshaft. Ultimately, I visited the office of this company situated on Kasturba Gandhi Marg, New Delhi. I met a lady company secretary and she informed me that this delay had taken place because they are engaged in streamlining the functioning of their company. One hundred shares, she said, were duplicate ones, a bad delivery and would have to be replaced. She assured me that this would be dispatched to me soon. When I repèatedly confronted her with the question that why the receipt of the shares were not acknowledged, she was evasive and could not give any satisfactory reply. Six weeks passed, nothing happened. Such is the state of transfers and registrations of newly acquired shares.

In all fairness to Reliance, the acknowledgement of receipt of my shares for transfer came within two months on a hand-written note, assuring me that the needful would be done soon. It lived upto its promise. My effort here is not to boost the prospects of any company, nor I am a great admirer of Reliance Group of Industries, after the episode of massive issuance of duplicate share, but my purpose is to state what has actually happened.

I am sure thousands of investors would have faced similar problems. I do not know what happens when a share is found to be a duplicate one and one is informed about it after six months of sending it for registration. I do not know if the broker or a sub-broker, in certain circumstances, would still be there, if he is not a credible one, to entertain such replacements.

4. Price Transparency

If an investor can claim that he has never felt his shares were sold at lower than the ruling market price or bought at higher price than the market value, he is one of an extremely rare breed. Lack of adequate information on the actual price at which the transaction took place has been a principal complaint of many investors. This is mainly because trading takes place in a ring where a common investor does not have an access, as a result he cannot know the exact price at which the deal was completed.

I had told my broker to purchase 500 shares of Chambal Fertilizers and Chemicals Ltd., not beyond the rate of Rs. 34 per share, but he booked the shares for me at the rate of Rs. 34.50. He told me that the shares could only be available at this rate. Next morning, when I saw the rate of the share in the newspapers it was Rs. 33.50. My protest to the broker did not produce any results. Over and above this, the broker charged me two per cent commission. I went through similar experience when I told him to sell my Reliance Petro Shares. I told my broker not to sell it at a rate lower than Rs. 17 per share. He sold it for Rs. 16, assuring me that this was the best rate he could get for me. The closing rate in the newspapers was Rs. 16.90.

Most of the time, the brokers seek your confirmation on sale and purchase of shares for you, but they are dishonest in their dealings and one has no means to check at what rate the actual deal has been negotiated.

5. Odd Lots

Odd lots of shares arising out of rights, bonus issues or otherwise, have in most case, been known to be quite illiquid. Except for a few financial institutions like Unit Trust of India, General Insurance Corporation of India and Canbank Financial Services, which accept odd lot shares only selectively, there are a few outlets where an investor can go for selling the odd lots. Even in cases where an investor might be able to sell his odd lots, the difference in price received for odd lots and market lots sometimes ran into more than 10 per cent of the sale value.

I had 100 shares of Hindustan Levers, the company gave bonus in the ratio of 2 shares for every 5 shares held. The 40 shares which I got were odd lots and despite repeated attempts, my broker could not sell the shares in the market. I had to sell them to an investment firm which dealt in odd lots at a discount of 10 per cent over the market price.

6. Delayed Transfers

Though regulations prescribe a maximum time limit of two months within which a company has to complete transfer formalities, in reality, this rarely happens. Most of us would have experienced receiving transferred share certificates several months late. Due to the inherent advantage of creating a shortage of shares in the market, managements have been known not to respond to complaints of investors.

Aditya sent 200 shares for transfer to ABC Ltd. He received them after five months. During this period, the price of this share had risen to Rs. 40 (when Aditya wanted to sell). It again fell to Rs. 27. Aditya could not capitalise on the opportunity to sell when he wanted to do so because of delay in transfer.

7. Lack of Information

Today any investor has to rely only on the scanty information dished out by a company either in the abridged prospectus or abridged annual report or through half-yearly results. Well-researched data is rarely available to an investor.

8. Delayed Refunds

The Companies Act, 1956 prescribes that allotment of refunds in case of public issues by companies should be completed within 10 weeks. However, companies have been known to issue pre-dated refund orders after even 4 to 5 months of the closure of the issue. As a result, an investor not getting any allotment, can at best, roll over his money just three times in a year.

During the first six months of 1992, the Securities and Exchange Board of India received 1,37,055 investor complaints of refund delays.

COMPANY RELATED PROBLEMS

1. Restricted Listing

Small/medium-sized companies resisted certain listing guidelines introduced in early 1989 which restricted listing on regular stock exchanges to companies with a minimum issued equity capital of Rs. 3 crores and a minimum public offer of equity capital of not less than Rs. 1.80 crores. This resulted in stifling the growth of smaller companies desiring to have public participation in its equity, as well as those which intended getting their shares listed on stock exchange.

2. High Issue Costs

The large number of bank collection centres (Minimum prescribed 558) all over the country which a company has to have at the time of rights/public issues have increased the issue costs to extremely high levels. The resultant heavy bank charges, advertising, printing and stationery costs which can run into 12 per cent to 15 per cent of the total issue, can be quite prohibitive in case of small companies or smaller issues.

3. Pricing of Issues

It is only recently that the new Sebi guidelines have permitted free pricing of capital issues. Till now, the administered pricing as regulated by the now abolished office of the Controller of Capital Issues (CCI), acted as a bane to several blue chip companies who could not price their shares as represented by fundamentals.

Regulated pricing used to lead, in most cases, to underpricing and occasionally to overpricing of securities. Underpricing led to heavy investor demand and resulted in multiple applications as well as heavy over-subscriptions. For genuine investors, such applications became like lotteries as chances of allotment were negligible.

The unofficial premiums which began to be quoted due to heavy demand for under-priced securities, broadly represented the difference between the true value of any security and the issue price. Amounts which should have rightfully gone to the company went to speculators who made multiple applications in fictitious names, a totally undesirable consequence.

Need for the OTC Exchange

It was with all the above in mind that OTC Exchange of India was set up to provide a comprehensive solution to these problems faced by companies and investors. From the point of view of development of a healthy and more orderly capital market in the country, taking into account the interest of investors on the one hand and rendering the market, efficient and cost effective for the issues on the other, the OTC Exchange was the answer.

The OTC Exchange of India is a company registered under the Companies Act, 1956. Its main objective is to set up and operate an Over the Counter Exchange in India which offers a nation-wide computerized, ringless and scripless trading facility to small investors in line with the most advanced global standards.

Formation of OTC Exchange

The OTC Exchange which became operational in November 1992 is a recognised stock exchange under Section 4 of the Securities Contracts (Regulations) Act. The OTCE has been jointly promoted by UTI, ICICI, IFCI, IDBI, LIC, GIC, SBI, Capital Markets and Canbank Financial Services.

Till September 1996, the OTCEI had 105 companies as its members and 270 dealers. It had 21 listed companies with a total market capitalisation of Rs. 170 crore. Only companies with an equity capital of Rs. 30 lakh to Rs. 25 crore are eligible for listing on the OTCEI. In addition, debentures with a total market capitalisation of Rs. 160 crore belonging to 12 companies were also listed and traded on the OTCEI. The OTCEI also permits trading in the equities of some highly liquid stocks and mutual funds listed on the Bombay Stock Exchange.

The main advantage of trading on the OTC Exchange is that it not only makes trading easier and quicker, but the trading mechanism is also investor-friendly, less volatile and provides for complete transparency in deals.

The other advantages are easier accessibility since the OTCEI plans to have a widely dispersed nationwide network of dealers, scripless trading, which means absence of cumbersome time-consuming transfer procedures, quicker payments, higher liquidity provided by market makers, lower jobbing spreads since the maximum allowable spread between buying and selling quotes cannot exceed three per cent and opportunities to buy scrips which quote at substantially lower P/E multiples those in the Bombay Stock Exchange. This exchange has its headquarters in Bombay.

OTCEI FEATURES

1. Investor Registration (IR)

All companies who want their security to trade have to compulsorily get registered with the OTC Exchange. This is simple, one time process, one can get registered either at the time of making an application for a public issue or at a later date when one wants to transact on the OTCEI secondary market whichever is earlier.

At the time of registration, the investor will get an INVEST OTC Card which would contain a registration number exclusive to the particular investor.

2. Ringless

Ringless trading helps in decentralising the location of the OTC counters, resulting in greater accessibility to the investor. Trading on the OTC Exchange takes place through a network of computers installed in the offices of the respective members/dealers who would be located at several places within the same city and across cities. The computers, through satellite and telephone lines, allow dealers to quote, query and transact using telecommunication links.

3. Computerised and Transparent

In the conventional stock exchanges an investor runs the risk of being misinformed on prices paid or secured for purchases or sales. The computerised OTC system is transparent with regard to the price and the time of trading and the amount retained as a brokerage.

4. Single Window Operation

For an investor, trading on the OTC Exchange is a single window operation. The investor can perform all security-related functions like transfer of shares, splitting and consolidation of shares, nomination, registering the power of attorney, besides actual trading, at any counter. Thus, instead of the investor running around to different market intermediaries, the respective counters are authorised to carry out all the above functions.

5. Faster Transfers and Trading Without Shares

Investors on the OTC Exchange will not generally trade with Share Certificates but with different tradable documents called the 'Counter Receipt' or the CR. When an investor gets allotment in a public issue, he would be sent a CR and not a share Certificate (SC). Similarly, when you purchase shares from any counter, you would receive a CR and not a SC.

The Investor is entitled to exercise the right of having the SC by surrendering the CR. But since the SC is not a tradable document, he would have to exchange it for a CR when he wants to trade. However, as the CR is a sufficient proof of ownership of the shares of a company, it is not necessary for an investor to exchange it against a share certificate unless otherwise required for any specific purpose.

Registrars for Companies on the OTC Exchange are allowed to transfer upto 0.5 per cent (per folio) of a company. This means that share transfers would be considerably quicker for smaller investors. But there are certain companies shares traded on OTC whose 'counter receipts' are not in existence and trading is of usual scripts.

6. Assured Liquidity

Investors would have come across instances where their broker tells them that a transaction could not be done because jobbers refused to give quotes. In the case of the OTC Exchange, such an instance is quite unlikely to arise. This is because the sponsor and the Additional Market Maker (terms explained later) have to compulsorily give both buy and sell quotes in a scrip at any point of time. This assures the investor of continuous liquidity of his investment at any point of time. More relevant is the fact that these market makers would also give quotes for odd lots of shares.

7. Faster Payments

Being a fully automated exchange employing facilities of registrars and custodians, any particular deal is completed in the shortest possible time. Hence payment for shares sold by an investor would normally be made within 2 to 3 days. At the same time, payment for shares purchased would have to be made immediately.

8. Nationwide Reach and Listing

The nationwide reach also enables widely dispersed trading, resulting in greater liquidity. Widely dispersed trading helps the investor in that he is likely to have a trading counter in the same locality thereby providing enhanced accessibility.

Similarly, presently, any company which comes out with a public issue has to indicate the stock exchanges in which it would be listed. It has also to pay listing fee to each of the exchanges where it intends to get enlisted. In the case of the OTC Exchange, which would have trading operations in several cities, companies would get listed on only one exchange, the OTC Exchange, enabling it to have nationwide listing.

9. Free Pricing

As per the guidelines issued by the Securities Exchange Board of India (SEBI), companies on regular stock exchanges, which do not fulfil the necessary track record criteria cannot issue shares at a premium. Their shares have to be issued at par. However, on the OTC Exchange, even in case of new companies without the necessary track record, where the shares of a company have been taken by the sponsor, they are allowed to be offered to the public at a later date at such price (*i.e.* even at a premium) as the sponsor may deem fit, subject to fulfilment of certain conditions.

Counter

The term counter refers to the location of the member or a dealer of the OTCEI where dealing actually takes place. On the OTC Exchange each counter acts as a trading floor. All the counters will trade in all the scrips listed on the OTC Exchange. At every counter, an investor can see the quotes on the PTI—OTC Scan, complete a transaction, as well as ask for investor services.

Members

Members on the OTC Exchange would only be financial institutions, scheduled banks and banking subsidiaries, Mutual Funds, Venture Capital Funds and Sebi approved merchant bankers and non-banking financial institutions. Members are essentially high net worth entities, with a minimum prescribed net worth of Rs. 2.5 crores. They are authorised to act as brokers for securities make market in scrips (*i.e.* quote both buy and sell prices for a declared number of securities), and act as a sponsor to companies. On the OTC Exchange, each company intending to go public, requires at least one sponsor. Under the sponsorship function, a member is required to:

(a) appraise the company's management capability,
(b) appraise the financial and technological viability of the company's project,
(c) value the scrip and determine the price,
(d) sponsor scrips to other members/dealers,
(e) hold scrip and later offer it to the public,
(f) arrange for an additional market-maker,
(g) perform all pre-issue post-issue functions for listing the company on the OTC Exchange and, above all,
(h) do compulsory market making in the issued scrip for at least three years from the date trading commences.

The process of sponsorship of scrips is intended to screen companies before listing them on the OTC Exchange giving investors better scrips to invest. For a member of OTCEI, being a sponsor means acting as a compulsory market maker in the particular scrip. In other words, the sponsor would be wedded to the company's scrip for at least three years.

Dealers

Dealers on the OTC Exchange may be individuals/partnership firms/corporate entities with a minimum specified net worth and necessary infrastructure to provide investors services. Dealers are allowed to act as brokers as well as make market in scrips.

Market Maker

A Market Maker (MM) on the OTC Exchange is somewhat akin to a jobber on the regular exchange. However, a market maker is a more regulated lot than a jobber, in that he has to compulsorily make market in a scrip for a minimum period. The principal differences between the two are as follows:

	Market Maker	*Jobber*
1.	Has to compulsorily give 2 way *i.e.* buy and sell quotes.	Cannot be compelled to offer 2 way quotes.
2.	Has to give minimum notice period of 6 days to the exchange for commencement and termination of market making.	Can commence and withdraw from jobbing at a moment notice.
3.	Has to take responsibility of making market compulsorily for 3 years/1 year/3 months.	Can do jobbing even for a day.

Market maker can be of 3 types.

(a) *Compulsory Market Maker (CMM)—sponsor*—As explained above, only a member is allowed to act as a sponsor and has to compulsorily make market in a scrip for at least three years continuously. Dealers cannot be CMM unless this function is assigned to them by the sponsor in that scrip. After a period of 3 years, the sponsor will continue to make market in the scrip till an alternative market maker is arranged for.

(b) *Additional Market Maker (AMM)*—An AMM can be either a member or a dealer of the OTCEI and would be appointed by the (CMM). The AMM has to make market in a scrip for at least One year continuously.

(c) *Voluntary Market Maker (VMM)*—Both Members and dealers can act as VMM on the OTC Exchange. A VMM has to make market in a scrip for at least 3 months continuously.

Settlor

The settlor acts as a record keeper of all documents and monitors the movements of the documents. The settlor keeps a record of the signatures of all investors for all the scrips. When an investor sells the shares, the CR is sent to the settlor for verification.

Registrar/Custodian

A registrar is an agent appointed by the company to perform the following functions:

(a) to transfer shares not exceeding 0.5 per cent per folio of the company's capital,
(b) to maintain a register of members,
(c) to keep in custody share certificates of the company to be exchanged with the CRS at the request of the investor.
(d) maintain complete record of signatures and other details and check the same when a CR and TD are received for transfer, and update the members register and signature records after effecting the transfer,
(e) inform respective counters on completion of the transfer/ formalities.
(f) registering power of attorney/transmission/transposition of shares/registering nominations, etc.

How Does an Investor Sell on the OTCEI

Like in the case of buy transaction, in case an investor wants to sell his shares on the OTC Exchange, the deal can either be 'direct deal' or a 'put—through deal'. In case of a direct deal, the investor does the transaction at the counter which is (a) a market maker in the particular scrip, and (b) is offering the best quota at that point of time. No brokerage is chargeable in case of a direct deal.

A put through deal is a transaction at any counter which is not a market maker in the particular scrip or is not quoting the best sale price at that point of time.

Steps—Steps in both cases are more or less the same, such as;

(a) Investor sees price on the PTI-OTC Scan, decides to sell.
(b) Investor checks with counter for best deals in terms of scrip price and quantity. Investor would also come to know whether it would be director put-through deal.
(c) Counter fills in investor details in the computer, if investor is willing to do the deal (either director or put-through)
(d) The counter queries OTC computer for best price available and quantity and informs investor.

Note—It may be noted that the quotation on the PTI-OTC Scan would only give an indicative price of a particular scrip.

However, the exact market price can be obtained only by querying the OTC Central Computer.

(a) Investor decides to make the deal-counter completes and confirms the deal as inventory is blocked in OTC Central Computer.
(b) Investor hands over his copy of the CR (signed now) alongwith duly signed transfer deed.
(c) Three copies of ScS (Sale confirmation Slip) printed out by counter, one copy is given to an investor, one copy is sent to market maker and one copy is kept by broker/dealer.
(d) CR and TD and a copy of the ScS sent to registrar/settlor.
(e) Settlor informs counter about CR genuineness and TD validity verification. Investor is given the cheque net of brokerage on production of the ScS.

When Does Seller Receive Payment

Payment for shares sold would normally be made within 3 to 4 days of the transaction. The CR along with the TD if required and ScS is sent to the settlor on the day of the sale. The settlor confirms the transaction after signature verification by comparison with the earlier copy of the PCR already sent when the investor has bought the shares. (PCR is a permanent counter receipt and has the same meaning as Counter Receipt).

On intimation to the counter (within a day or two), the counter has to make the payment to the investor. If the investor has an account in the designated bank, he can receive the credit for the same immediately.

What is the Validity Period of the CR

As matters stand today there is no time limit for expiry of the CR.

How Shares are Transferred

There would be no change in the transfer deed (TD) from what is prevalent today, but the process of transfer would be slightly different. Instead of the buyer and seller both signing on the same TD (as in the case now), the seller would sign on the seller's part of one TD and the buyer would sign on the buyer's part in another TD. Both TDs would be sent by the investors (through their respective countries) to the registrar where the matching is done and the transfer effected. Following this, the registrar intimates the counter about the transfer having been effected and the counter in turn intimates the investor.

Since the registrars have been authorised by companies to transfer shares on its behalf, shares upto 0.5 per cent per folio, of the total issued capital of the company would be immediately transferred by them. The time limit fixed for such transfer is 7 days.

In case of a larger lot of shares, they would have to be sent to the company for transfer and it would have to return them duly transferred within 18 days.

The OTCEI has prescribed strict guidelines for compliance of the rules laid down for the settlor as well as the company. Heavy penalties are prescribed for non-compliance.

The OTCEI was heralded a few years back as the best thing that happened to our stock markets for decades. It was marketed by the government and its own executives as a manna from heaven for smaller companies who did not wish to expose themselves to the harsh realities of the major sources.

Further, the 'bought out' deal was perceived as a mechanism to put premium money into the hands of entrepreneurs, rich in project skills but low on capital.

A phenomenal infrastructure was built up. Today, the OTC empire extends to 45 cities, boasts of 150 sponsors and 1,000 dealers. But it has become a ghost exchange and exists more in newspapers columns than in trading volume.

If one estimates is to be received, Reliance trades more value in one day in the main exchanges than the OTC exchange as a whole in one year.

This pathetic state has led to mass resignation of its top management in search of greener pastures.

OTCEI Performance

The following reasons can be given for the poor performance of this exchange:

1. This exchange was promoted by the Government of India through its eight largest financial institutions who own the OTCEI. Rs. 10 crore was put in as the seed money by UTI, ICICI, IFCI, IDBI, GIC, LIC, SBI Caps and Canbank Financial Services. Today, these promoters have forgotten about the exchange. Apart from the seed capital given at the time of inception, no other help has been given by these institutions to the exchange nor they take interest in its day-to-day operation.
2. The exchange is plagued by lack of liquidity and depth. Investors find it difficult to get out of large chunk of shares, a single large deal swings the market. The major reason for this is the lack of high net worth players on the exchange.

   On April 30, 1996, the Securities and Exchange Board of India (SEBI) permitted trading of an additional 217 scrips on the OTCEI. The move was expected to increase the much needed liquidity in the scrips that are listed on the exchange but as yet its activity is very small in terms of volume and value.

   The List includes Group A scrips of the Bombay Stock Exchange (BSE). The permitted scrips include ACC, Arvind Mills, Brooke Bond, IPCL, ITC, TISCO, NOCIL, Siemens, Videocon and BSES. There are already 105 scrips that are permitted to be traded on the OTCEI.

   According to the OTCEI official, the move should boost the volumes on the exchange tremendously. "OTC has reached in 42 big cities across the country and the Sebi move will target the retail investor".

   There has been mixed reactions from the broker community to Sebi's decision. According to a OTCEI broker, the expansion of the permitted securities list will not help the exchange attract more liquidity. This view is because operations on it are small and they cannot compete with NSE and BSE.

   The investors have lost interest in the already permitted scrips because there are problems like bad delivery attached to the permitted securities as the exchange cannot intervene in the trading of these scrips. The present trading software and hardware are not efficient enough to allow more scrips to be included for trading. Moreover, if the BSE is allowed to expand its operations into other cities, why should an investor go to the OTCEI? They will go in for an exchange that provides price effectiveness. If the volume is more, trading will be more, which means maximum prices, which is provided by the BSE and NSE.

3. The Exchange has introduced new concepts in the Indian capital markets that are ahead of time, like transaction plus trading cycle, market making of scrips.
4. Market Making concept has failed for two reasons. First, Market-Making calls for substantial holding power, something that most, if not all, market makers lack. Second, in the absence of sustained investor interest and an active secondary market in the scrip, market makers will just not be able to off-load their holding, except at a loss.

   The unique selling point of OTCEI has been its market-making concept. According to the rules, the compulsory market maker has to give a two-way quote (buy and sell) for the first 18 months and the additional market maker for the first 12 months from the date of listing.

   There seems to be little respect for this rule amongst the market makers if the recent happenings are any indication. It began with Rasuvishi Plastic, an OTCEI-listed company, which saw no sell quotes during the first few trading days in the month of January 1996. The market makers said that they were unable to give sell quotes because they had exhausted all their stock.

   The exchange rules state that in the case of such an eventuality, the market maker will have to purchase shares from the market and offer sell quotes afresh.

   Also, at the time of the issue, a minimum of 5 per cent of the issued capital has to be picked up by the market makers. Though there is no monitoring of the stock thereafter, the market maker has to maintain some inventory to be able to give two-way quotes in the script. But the market makers did not make any serious attempt to pick up stock from the market. The buy quote given by them was ridiculously low. Since no one was ready to sell at those prices, they could not buy any equity.

This caught the OTCEI management unawares. Mr. Ajeet Prasad, Managing Director, OTCEI, said that it was the first time that they were facing a situation like this. They could not force the market maker to give a more realistic buy quote so as to be able to pick up stock from the market. It is felt that the lack of any serious action from the exchange may prompt other market makers to follow suit. Already there have been no sell quotes of Veer Vardhman Textile Mills. Another couple of companies were added to the list on April 9, 1996. These are Absolute Aromatics, Shetkari Solvents and Dewas Metal Sections.

The Delhi Stock Exchange's (DSE) has also proposed to make market-making compulsory for all scrips that have not been traded for the past one year. The suggestion can at best be described as utopian. The scheme though ideal on paper, is hard to implement in practice. The DSE must learn from the experiment of the OTCEI.

The proposal reportedly envisages companies engaging jobbers who undertake to provide continuous two-way quotes for the shares in question. The idea is to provide investors who have bought shares in companies in which there is no trading on the exchange—and there are many such companies—with a ready exit option.

Since the biggest impediment to successful market-making is the lack of adequate finance, the exchange is also trying to finalise a line of credit package for these jobers as well. However, well-intentioned the DSE's proposal, given the difficulties, it is unlikely to be successful. Moreover, beyond a point, it is not for the exchange to protect the investor from himself. Investors who put their hard-earned money in dubious companies must be prepared to suffer.

5. The BSE and the NSE are both known to have large volumes of trade due to speculation. If one were to take the percentage of the aggregate delivery volumes to the total market capitalisation of these SEs, it would form less than 0.1 per cent. As against this, speculative trading volumes (not resulting in physical delivery of shares) would constitute almost 0.6 per cent of the aggregate market capitalisation.

This indicates that speculation forms an integral part of any SE functioning which would otherwise see pathetic volumes. Even an investor's psyche the world over is geared more to speculation rather than investment-oriented purchases.

Considering the above facts, it is indeed difficult to fathom why, neither the OTCEI nor Sebi has thought it fit to introduce some form of speculation on the exchange.

The best option could be the NSE version of intra settlement speculation with the introduction of options and fixtures eventually. This would take the form of a weekly settlement system for the OTCEI's listed and permitted segment of securities trading.

6. The slump in the stock market during the period 1995-96 due to the political uncertainty hit OTCEI hard. Whatever interest the investors showed in this exchange in late 1994, dried up totally as there are much better opportunities in the known BSE blue chips, many of which traded at their lowest.
7. Last, but one of the most important reasons is the management of the exchange which is highly centralised and bureaucratic.

The State Financial Corporations (SFCs) have decided not to sponsor companies on the OTCEI unless the exchange effects basic changes in its trading system, and the promoter financial institutions agree to support issues on the OTCEI.

The SFCs want the system of trading through counter receipts (CRs) should be done away with and should be replaced with the normal system of trading through physical certificates. Investors do not prefer to leave the certificates with the sub-brokers and allow them to do all the trading for them. They say that the concept of CRs is investor-unfriendly.

SFC officials want the spread between buy and sell quotas, presently limited to 10 per cent, bc allowed to go higher, in case the scrip is not attracting voluntary market makers. They demand that the 10 per cent limit be applicable only to scrips that have voluntary market makers. They point out that if the public issue is to survive, institutional participation is essential.

The biggest drawback is the dependence on electronic system. It relied on telephone lines which frequently breakdown the communication links through Vsat in the case of NSE.

To sum up, if the OTCEI is to survive the turmoil it is presently passing through, the changing of the settlement cycle is one of the immediate measures needed to transform it into a more buoyant system or else this advanced national exchange could find itself in a position worse than the small regional exchanges.

Sebi appointed a Committee on April 17, 1996 to review the working of the OTCEI. The Committee, consisting of 15 members, was chaired by Mr. S.A. Dave, the former chairman of Unit Trust of India and OTC.

The Committee, the first of its kind in the Exchange's history, looked at a gamut of issues and problems plaguing the exchange.

Besides Mr. Dave, the panellists comprised Mr. Nipun Mehta and Mr. Mahesh Thakkar, representing the dealer segment, Mr. Kayu Mehta of Tata Investment Corporation and Mr. O.P. Srivastava of SCICI from the member group. The financial institutions, IDBI, UTI, and SIDBI nominated their own representatives on the panel.

The Committee, included representatives from the dealers and member segments, financial institutions, other exchanges and industry representatives.

While the other exchanges were represented by Mr. Ravi Narain of the National Stock Exchange and Mr. J.J. Bhatt of the BSE, the industry representatives consisted of Magnum Intermediates, represented by Mr. P.C. Surana, and Maxwell Apparels, represented by Mr. L.J. Reddy. The panel also consisted of Mr. R. Ravi Mohan of Crisil, the erstwhile Chief Executive of the OTC Exchange of India.

The Member-Secretary of the Committee was Mr. O.P. Gahrotra, Senior Executive Director, Mr. R.D. Joshi of the Department of Company Affairs, was also on the panel.

Despite the appointment of Mr. Dave as Chairman of the panel, a section of OTC members felt that getting NSE Managing Director, Mr. R.H. Patil, to play a role in it would have been a better idea.

Recommendations of Dave Committee

The Dave Committee made the following sweeping recommendations on September 7, 1996 to boost OTCEI.

The committee pulled up the exchange promoters, the FIs for not actively participating in the exchange. It has pointed out that the absence of institutional players has led to a vacuum in the exchange as the market makers do not have an exit route. The report suggested that institutional participation would drive greater market participation and improve price realisation.

The committee has suggested the strengthening of management structure and manpower as well as upgrading of infrastructure and technology within the OTCEI.

In a major effort to attract new companies into the OTCEI fold, the Committee suggested that companies not having a three-year dividend-paying record or who have not been appraised and funded by institutions should be allowed to raise funds by listing on the OTCEI, provided they fulfil OTCEI's criteria.

All companies, irrespective of their size be enlisted on the OTCEI, like in other exchange in the country.

Bought-out deals, which may not fulfil the three-year dividend-paying record or the institutional appraisal and funding criteria, may be allowed the facility of a sale offer, listing and trading only on the OTCEI.

In a major NASDAQ-style move, the Committee recommended that the equity shares of unlisted companies, that is privately-placed shares with institutional investors be allowed to trade on OTCEI. This would facilitate inter-institutional trades and placement of shares with FIIs who have now been permitted to subscribe to unlisted company stocks.

In a shareholder-friendly move, the Committee did away with the minimum share holding requirement (Five shareholders for every Rs. 1 lakh capital) applicable on other bourses.

Thus, companies facing delisting on other exchanges because of this factor or not being able to tap the market, would find the OTCEI a welcome avenue.

Recognising the problems of paucity and lack of access to funds, the Committee has recommended a graded approach to the market maker's inventory of stock.

Earlier, a market maker had to hold 5 per cent of the companies issued capital irrespective of the total market capitalisation. The Committee has suggested that the market makers can hold 5 per cent for a capital holding of less than Rs. 5 crores, 2 per cent between Rs. 5 and Rs. 10 crores. This move, it is felt, will considerably reduce the funding need of market makers and encourage sponsors to take up more makret making assignments.

Further, recognising the glitches involved in arranging finance for settling trades, the Committee recommended a shift from T + 3 system to T + 5 settlement system where the pay-in takes place on day five and the pay-out on day six.

However, it is said the exchange should revert to the T + 3 system when the banking system is suitably geared up.

Both the NSE and the OTCEI are promoted by the same set of institutions. Mr. Dave suggested that the NSE and the OTCEI ought to work together to arrive at synergies.

In short, the Dave Committee's suggestions can be summed up as follows:

1. All companies with post-issue equity below Rs. 10 crores be listed on the OTCEI.
2. Shift from T + 3 settlement system to T + 5.
3. Scrap upper limit of Rs. 25 crores to list on OTCEI.
4. Companies facing development should refund money to shareholders.
5. Offers for sale for BODs only through OTCEI.
6. Equity of unlisted shares be allowed to trade on OTCEI.
7. Separate listed scrip category for scrip delisted from other SEs.
8. Sebi should allow the OTC to increase companies under the permitted securities and permitted debentures segment.
9. Paid-up capital upto Rs. 10 crores will attract market making provisions. Endorsement of the Malgam Committee proposal of listing all scrips with less than Rs. 10 crores paid-up capital on OTCEI.
10. Promoting institutions should play a more active role in underwriting issues for the primary market.
11. Rs. 50 to Rs. 100 crores promoter institution fund proposed for investment in OTC scrips.

OTCEI Move to Improve Functioning

On December 18, 1996, the OTCEI board approved a number of measures to improve the functioning of the exchange. Among the major decisions taken were the transferability of membership, relaxation of market making norms and two-way trading of partly paid shares.

Making the dealership card transferable, as on other exchanges, has been the long standing demand of the dealers. This shall give an escape route to a number of dealers who have not activated their counters. It would also help shift membership out of the hands of dormant members to dealers willing to deal on the exchange.

The requirement for the compulsory market maker (CMM) and the additional market maker (AMM) to continue giving two-way quotas even after the expiry of the 18-months and 12-months period has been done away with. Now, trading after the expiry of the initial 18-months listing period shall be order driven. However, dealers shall be free to give quotes as voluntary market makers in scrips of their choice.

The Board has also given its approval to the graded system of market making as recommended by the Dave Committee. As a regret, market making inventory between the CMM and the AMM shall be graded according to the company's market capitalisation.

Trading between market makers has been approved. Till now, market makers were not allowed to trade amongst themselves and the only way for them to execute deals was in the name of fictitious clients. Two-way trading of partly paid shares has also been allowed. Earlier, the market makers could buy from the market but could not sell partly paid scrips. As a result, they were forced to hold on to large inventory.

Keeping in mind the sharp fluctuations in prices of some scrips, the OTCEI Board has prescribed certain band widths for inter-day (closing price of a day and the opening price of the following day) and intra-day price movements.

For a price range of less than Rs. 10, the inter-day band width is 6 per cent and intra-day 24 per cent, for price range of Rs. 10-50, 5 per cent and 20 per cent, for a price range of

Rs. 50-100, 4 per cent and 16 per cent and for a scrip price in excess of Rs. 100, 3 per cent and 12 per cent.

The Board has also prescribed a corporate action breaker which will be applicable for 30 minutes immediately after any information having any bearing on a particular company's price is announced.

The Board has also okayed trading in open-ended Birla Mutual Fund.

6

Price Rigging

Speculation is as much a part of the stock market as is investment. As the market matures, it is no longer considered quite as dirty a word as it once was. But, in the wrong hands it can still be a mighty destructive tool, particularly, in a market going through a rather painful transition.

What is Price Rigging

Price rigging is usually generic to certain species of scrips, essentially of companies with low equity and low floating stock. The most common kind of rigging is the one that shows up a few months before a company approaches the capital market. The M S Shoes case is a classical example. Surprisingly, it is found that this is more true for financial services companies, which are more aggressive in approaching the capital market for money.

Circular trading is the most common route for rigging prices. Some scrips which witnessed high volumes in 1995 at the BSE, include Rupangi Impex, G.R. Magnets, Surlux Health, Ascent Capital, Panch Cement and Arpan Leasing. In fact, these scrips had made it to the list of top 20 traded shares.

Often, companies wanting to place their shares with financial institutions (FIs) or foreign institutional investors (FIIs) also jack up share prices. After maintaining an inflated price for a few months, they then place the equity with the FI or FIIs. But, soon after the scrip slides back to more realistic levels. Analysts observing this phenomenon closely say that institutions have lost money on such transactions.

The grey market, of course, is always there. It's a market where unofficial premiums are lucrative indeed. Take an example, company 'X' is coming with a public issue; to get the issue subscribed, or even oversubscribed, the management activates the grey market.

This is done through a network of operators who start buying the shares of company X at a premium from other operators who are confident that the initial listing price of the scrip will be less than the price at which company is ready to buy its share at that moment.

Soon enough, company X buys as many shares as are proposed under the issue or even more. To give delivery of scrip which he has short sold, the operator subscribes to the issue for as many shares he has shortsold. Or, if he expects the issue to be over-subscribed twice, he applies for twice the amount he has shortsold. That's just what the company wanted!

The company keeps the expected subscription a closely guarded secret. Since there are a number of operators who have shortsold the scrip and have applied to the issue, it usually gets heavily over-subscribed. In some cases it has even touched a figure of 100 times. Obviously then, the operator gets less shares than what he shortsold.

To cover his position the operator who was earlier a seller turns a buyer, pushing the scrip's price up. A good example is Tobu Enterprises' issue. It was over-subscribed 150 times, which people close to the market, attribute to grey market operations. The scrip opened at Rs. 30 and slipped to Rs. 12 in just a few days.

What happens when issues are not fully subscribed, a fairly common occurence during early 1995? Though officially not declared devolved, large applications are generally put in either on the last date or even after the issue is closed. The operators who bail out the company charge the prevailing interest rate on the amount they put in or work out an agreement with the company who buys back the allotted scrips at a pre-decided price.

As genuine subscription is nominal, the promoters are in a hurry to recover their costs. So, in most such cases, the issue opens below par and what little liquidity there is because of some genuine subscription, is mopped up by the operators as people resort to distress selling.

In instances where the operator is unable to mop up liquidity in the market, the company normally holds up the transfer of shares or else takes its own sweet time in converting partly paid-up shares to fully paid-up, thus reducing liquidity in the market. This is the opportune time to spread rumours that the scrip is going to rise and smaller, gullible investors who have little information fall back on clamour to buy the scrip being offloaded by the operators.

In a bearish market, dubious rallies by scrips is fueled not because of covering by short sellers but because promoters enter the market with specific intention of manipulating price.

There are any number of cases that have gone unnoticed because the promoter has consciously kept his issue on low key. Only statutory advertisement requires under law are given. Stationery is not supplied to any broker except the stock exchange, and that too limited. The promoter puts in the entire amount of the issue through a few applications in the name of relatives, friends or corporate bodies owned by him. Thus, he is able to corner all the liquidity without incurring any cost for manipulation. The only cost he incurs is on issue expenses which in any case are nominal because there has been no publicity. After the issue closes, the promoters start circular trading and with every increase in prices offload a part of their holding. This rise continues till they are able to offload all shares they want to.

Price Performance

Price movements give a fair idea of whether a particular scrip is being manipulated or not. And, there are even a few common characteristics one can watch out for. Drawing a trendline on the price and volume charts you will notice that there is generally a parabolic increase in price and volume. In most cases, after the price touches a new high combined with new peak volumes, the price crashes suddenly without any support at lower levels and volumes fall dramatically as well.

The reason for the parabolic increase in volume and prices is that the operator who has already mopped up liquidity starts offloading his position to either short sellers or small investors with every increase in price. As soon as the scrip touches a new high, the operator offloads his entire position, and neither the small investor nor the short seller is in a position to absorb the selling pressure. This leads to crash in price either the very next day or within a few days of such new highs.

This is exactly what happened in scrips like SPS Data Products, Xedd Telecom, Indo-American Optics and Toor Spinner. These scrips shot up with large volumes being traded, and soon after reaching a new peak, crashed. When such scrips are listed, they are normally below par or just about at par.

Another example, Nepa Paper Ltd. came out with public issue in June 1995 but the response was lackadaisical. After listing, the scrip moved within the range of Rs. 10-12 until the first week of October 1995. Initially, the operator mopped up liquidity and the scrip touched a high of Rs. 20 by mid-October. Weak on fundamentals and technicals, some operators short sold the scrip.

In this race between the bears and bulls, the bulls had more financial muscle and were able to absorb all the selling pressure up to a price of Rs. 20. Just when the bears thought the scrip had reached as high as it could, the bulls pulled it up further and the bears scrambled to cover their positions. This saw price shot up from Rs. 23 to Rs. 70 in a short span of 13 days. At this point, Sebi finally woke up and asked the stock exchange to probe the incident. All exchanges then suspended trading in the scrip.

In most cases, when trading is resumed after such a ban, prices nosedive and the investors who have entered at higher levels are either forced to book heavy losses or remain struck with the shares.

There have been signs of just this happening in scrips such as Kuber Floritech, Radhika Spinning, Adeshwar Cotton and Century Extrusions, suggesting that operators are showing undue interest in these scrips.

Price Rigging by MS Shoes

MS Shoes East Ltd. was involved in the most prominent case of price rigging in 1995. The Company was incorporated in 1986. It is engaged in the manufacture of leather shoes and footwear components and exports all its wares mainly to Australia and Western Europe.

The Company's turnover shot up from Rs. 3.12 crores in 1986-87 to Rs. 116.61 crores in 1993-94 and touched Rs. 200 crores mark in 1994-95.

In 1994, the company's Managing Director, Mr. Pavan Sachdeva, drew up an ambitious diversification strategy to enter several new areas like hotels, steel, liquor and yarn. His plans included the setting up of an integrated spinning unit for the manufacture of cotton and filament yarn as well as the construction of a 5-star deluxe guest house complex in New Delhi along with other hotels in Agra, Mussoorie, Shimla and Jaipur.

He had chalked up an impressive list of foreign tie-ups. He signed an MoU with an internationally reputed Intercontinental Hotel chain; claimed to have entered into a buy-back agreement with Marubeni, the Japanese Trading major and also planned to tie-up with Inver-Gordon, the UK-based liquor company.

In September 1994, Mr. Sachdeva bagged HUDCO's prime hotel land in South Delhi under controversial circumstances. He decided to enter the capital market with a Rs. 699.57 crores public-cum-rights issue with a high profile media campaign. In December 1994, he announced the public issue of Rs. 428 crores fully convertible debentures (FCD) to finance the hotel and yarn projects.

On February 11, 1995, *The Economic Times* revealed that MS Shoes price of Rs. 699.57 is cum-rights and was expected to drop sharply after public issue. This fact was not revealed by the company.

The TV advertisements of the issue mentioned the cum-rights price instead of ex-rights price, and thus began the chain of events which culminated in the arrest of Mr. Sachdeva.

Mr. Sachdeva was charged with massive rigging of his share. The MS Shoes issue spurted from Rs. 145 to Rs. 250 on the Bombay Stock Exchange. This is despite the fact the scrip was available between Rs. 137 to Rs. 142 on the National Stock Exchange.

The BSE remained closed for three days from March 20, 1995 to March 22, facing one of the worst financial crisis as one of the brokers of MS Shoes, R.S. Jhaveri, defaulted in payment of Rs. 18 crores. The default took place due to the clubbing of settlements. According to the Securities Exchange Board of India's (SEBI) guidelines, all transactions in shares had to be settled after a week.

In a landmark development, Sebi had issued a show-cause notice to MS Shoes for buying its own shares. In addition, Sebi also decided to prosecute the company on the charges of misleading the investors.

This is for the first time that any company was charged with buying its own shares. The Sebi prosecution for misleading investors is also the first against any company. Sebi disclosed that it had written to the Department of Company Affairs (DCA) to take action against MS Shoes for purchase of its own shares, a violation of Company's Act.

The MS Shoes composite right-cum-public issue was later cancelled and the company was asked to refund subscriptions. The period before the issue had seen the share price register a spectacular rise.

SBI Capital Markets, which was lead manager of the MS Shoes issue, is also to take its share of the blame. It was the lead manager which had to vet the prospectus with due diligence. It ought to have been aware of the Sebi guidelines relating to public issue proceeding a rights issue. How, then did it give a due diligence certificate to MS Shoes? SBI Capital is the largest merchant banker and if it is allowed to make such mistakes without any punitive action, won't the others use it as a precedent? Moreover, it was reported that SBI Capitals had sold 60,050 shares of MS Shoes itself. This warranted an investigation into insider trading.

The Central Bureau of Investigation (CBI) arrested Mr. Pavan Sachdeva, on the charges of entering into a criminal conspiracy with three Sebi and two SBI Caps officials to chast investors.

The main charge against Mr. Sachdeva and MS Shoes East is that they cheated investors by violating Sebi guidelines for their Rs. 699 crores rights-cum-public issues, and rigging of share prices. Officials of Sebi and SBI Caps were charged for assisting him in the deed.

The CBI filed the first information report (FIR) with the Delhi Special Police Establishment and Bombay on April 4 against Mr. Sachdeva and the officials. This was followed up with raids in Bombay and Delhi. Besides Mr. Sachdeva, six others who were charged for criminal conspiracy were Mr. M.D. Patel, Executive Director of Sebi; Ms Uma Narayanan, Divisional Chief, Sebi; Mr. R. Mohan, officer in Sebi; Mr. P.S. Mehrotra, General Manager, SBI Caps; Ms. Neetika Juneja, Manager, SBI Caps and MS Shoes East Ltd.

The FIR charged Sebi and SBI Caps, which lead-managed the Rs. 699-crores right-cum-public issue for vetting the faulty prospectus.

According to the FIR, the three Sebi officials, "knowingly approved the vetting of the prospectus and offer documents of MS Shoes". The two SBI Caps officers omitted to mention a number of breaches of the guidelines in the prospectus and offer documents and issued a false certificate.

This breach, the FIR pointed out, of Sebi guidelines was done in many ways. Sebi guidelines stipulate that the gap between a rights and a public issue should not exceed more than 30 days. However, Mr. Sachdeva and MS Shoes Ltd. were permitted to breach these guidelines by Sebi officials—Mr. Patel, Ms. Narayanan and Mr. Mohan.

According to the CBI report, investors compared the issue price with the cum-rights price, while the correct comparison should have been with the ex-rights price, which would have been substantially lower.

Secondly, the three Sebi officials, pointed out the FIR, waived the stipulation of 30 days difference between the rights and the public issue. They allowed the company a gap of a minimum 90 days (the rights issue was planned to commence in April 1995), which provided it a potential chance for diverting the public issue proceeds for subscribing to the rights entitlements of the promoters, which was about Rs. 130 crores.

In addition, the three Sebi officials did not take any steps to instruct the company to prominently display the exact ex-rights price with reference to market quotations. The CBI charged that "the three Sebi officials had no authority to deviate from these guidelines as there was no provision in the Sebi Act.

The CBI pointed that a Sebi official Mr. Mohan, while making comprehensive written queries on various aspects of the offer documents, did not point out the said discrepancies.

"The entire question of waiving this condition was suspicoiusly completed in a period of three working days and only a suspicious verbal back reference was made to the lead managers in the intervening period."

While the lead manager, SBI Capital Markets informed that the rights issue was underwritten, Sebi officials did not seek details of the underwritten before vetting the offer. They also did not give any instruction to the Delhi Stock Exchange not to release the proceeds of public issue till the entire rights issue was subscribed to prevent diversion of funds.

Despite the fact that Mr. Patel was subsequently made aware through criticism in the Press (the *Economic Times* dated February 11) and also through a letter from a Sebi board member, he did not instruct the lead managers to specifically mention the ex-rights price on the basis of a definite calculation based on stock exchange quotations of various dates.

The waiving of the 30-days stipulation was further irregular as guidelines have catered to the contingency as brought forth as an excuse by Mr. Sachdeva, of pending debenture conversion by stimulating reservation of such shares to be allotted after the conversion date, and the officials knowingly avoided to consider the same.

Sebi's Action

The three Sebi officials also allowed Mr. Sachdeva with the assistance of Mr. Mehrotra and Ms. Juneja (SBI Caps officials) to collect 50 per cent subscription on the application whereas Sebi guidelines clearly stipulate that where on application and on allotment if an amount of more than Rs. 250 crore is to be collected, not more than 25 per cent should be collected on application.

Despite the fact this composite issue was of Rs. 699 crores, Mr. Sachdeva and his company was permitted to collect 50 per cent of price on application. This had the potential for diversion of funds for subscribing to the promoters rights issue later. This also became possible as the Sebi officials had already permitted him to breach the 30 days stipulation.

As per Sebi guidelines, in case of fully convertible debentures one-third of the issue amount should be subscribed by the promoters to the equity, alternatively they should subscribe to 20 per cent of the proposed debenture issue.

This condition was allowed to be breached. As per the Sebi guidelines, the promoters have to bring in their contribution before the opening of the public issue, which should be 20 per cent of the total issue capital.

Since the total issue capital was inclusive of the share premium, the promoters are required to subscribe to that extent. However, the promoters of MS Shoes, who had subscribed to a large number of shares earlier at cheap rates, were allowed to reckon these shares bought at cheap rates a few months earlier, anticipating a heavy premium issue for the purpose of promoters quota.

In this way, the three Sebi and SBI Caps officials exempted Mr. Sachdeva from bringing the promoters quota of Rs. 85.65 crores.

The Sebi officials also permitted MS Shoes to deviate from the stipulated format under the heading (Capital Structure). The Sebi guidelines, vide circular No. 7 (1993-94) dated January 20, 1994, stipulate that each head should have:

- Number of instruments.
- Description.
- Aggregate nominal value.
- Issue amount.

But MS Shoes was allowed to dispense with the issue amount because they did not want the public to know the aggregate amount of money first contributed to the issue capital (not nominal value), and had they done so, they could have got exposed of the fact the promoters contribution was insufficient. To further facilitate the deception, Sebi and SBI Cap officials permitted MS Shoes to further dispense with the stipulation of disclosure pertaining to promoters contribution under the head 'notes'.

Here again the promoters were permitted to withhold the details of the issue price and percentage to the total issue capital despite clear provisions in guidelines that these should be mentioned in offer documents.

The guilt of Sebi officials in their conspiracy with the SBI Caps officials and Mr. Sachdeva was seen from the fact that a very comprehensive back reference detailing a large number of queries was made by Sebi on December 21, 1994, after intensive scrutiny of offer documents.

However, such apparent and important guidelines having grave consequences were not even mentioned though it was their bounden duty to do so.

In addition, it was brought to the notice of Sebi officials that the promoters had issued backdated shares at a price of Rs. 50 per share, which was done after the Sebi guidelines of August 4, 1994, mandating promoters to buy shares at market rates was brought to force. The Sebi officials did not make any efforts to verify the sale before the opening of the public issue.

The FIR also stated that the lead manager of SBI Caps had indulged in insider trading with a large number of shares of the company with the purpose of rigging the price to deceive the generally ignorant investor.

Probe into VABAL Misuse by MS Shoes

Even as Mr. Sachdeva was arrested, the Directorate General of Foreign Trade (DGFT) instituted an inquiry against the group company of controversy-marred MS Shoes (East) Ltd. (MSSEL), for allegedly misusing its value-based advance licence (VABAL).

The licence, issued in February 1993, was for importing large quantities of synthetic rubber (acrylonitrile butadiene rubber or NBR) valued at Rs. 19.71 crores (CIF). Against this, the company undertook an obligation to export Rs. 27.60 crores worth of synthetic rubber sheets.

But in the transactions that followed, the company, MS International Ltd. (MSIL), is alleged to have over-invoiced the value of its exports to get much higher VABAL entitlement. It was also charged with presenting a "bogus export order" to the DGFT for exports made against VABAL.

According to a Commerce Ministry official, a reference is being made to the Indian Mission in Dubai for establishing the antecedents of M/s. Taj Al Khaleej General Trading (TAKGT)—the trading firm which MSIL is said to have contracted to export synthetic rubber sheets valued at Rs. 27.60 crores.

"We are also once again looking at the company's records to establish charges of over-invoicing of exports," the official added.

As regards another allegation that imported synthetic rubber was being illegally diverted to the domestic market, the official said relevant records of the company were examined. But at that time "they were all right".

Nevertheless, depending on the feed-back the Commerce Ministry gets from the Indian Mission abroad, these records may be examined once again, he added.

It has been further brought to the notice of DGFT that the VABAL issued to MSIL disallowed the company from importing one of the raw materials (high density polypropylene of HDPE). But despite this, the value of VABAL remained the same, instead of decreasing proportionately to the value of HDPE.

Moreover, the company was also charged with having imported large quantities of NBR at much lower prices, but not used the requisite quantities of the material in the exported synthetic rubber sheets.

In a related development during June 1994, the Central Bureau of Investigation conducted a simultaneous raid in Delhi, Bombay and Calcutta on several companies that were suspected to have misused VABAL and avoided payment of taxes/duties. The raid included the premises of the MS Shoes group as well.

The raids were conducted on a specific suspicion that certain firms had been purchasing dollars from the *havala* market and over-invoicing their exports for obtaining higher VABAL entitlements. But at the same time, in order to meet their export obligations goods were being sold to agents abroad.

MSIL belongs to a group of companies, which includes MS Shoes (East) Ltd, Universal Exports and Pearl International Ltd. The group is headed by Mr. Sachdeva.

MS Shoes case is still pending in the court. Meanwhile, SBI Capital Markets has been exonerated of the charges filed by Sebi against it. The penalty imposed by Sebi in the form of three-months suspension of the SBI Caps has also been quashed.

In MS Shoes case, a single-man appellate authority, set up by the Ministry of Finance had, in a 26-page order, held that "events which could not be anticipated could not be prevented", and thus SBI Caps was not guilty.

Sebi had imposed a suspension on SBI Caps for failing to exercise due diligence in the MS Shoes public offering in

February 1995. The appellate authority said that SBI Caps "had no means to anticipate and so could not prevent, and hence cannot be accused of negligence." The authority also noted that Sebi itself had given certain relaxations while clearing the issue.

Sebi had charged that SBI Caps had failed to ensure that the MS Shoes obtained the merchant banker's approval for advertisements issued by it and had failed to restrain the company from issuing the 'misleading' advertisement.

To this, the appellate authority observed: "It is difficult to believe that SBI Caps had not taken any action in this regard. For minor lapses, Sebi's own guidelines provide for giving warning and penal action. Sebi should have warned SBI Caps instead of imposing such a harsh punishment."

MS Shoes Loses Hotel Plots

On April 12, 1996, the Delhi High Court allowed the Housing and Urban Development Corporation (HUDCO) to reauction the MS Shoes promoter, Mr. Sachdeva's five-star hotel plot in Andrews Ganj, New Delhi. It also dismissed the company's appeal for more time to pay the second instalment for the plot.

With this court order, MS Shoes lost all the money it had put into the two plots. The amount involved was Rs. 74-crores for the guest house plot and Rs. 50-crores for the hotel plot. It has already been stated that its public issue was devolved and it was asked to refund money to the public.

SEBI Crackdown on 50 Brokers for Price Rigging

The Securities and Exchange Board of India conducted on July 7, 1996, its biggest nationwide investigation into capital market-related offences. In this case six small cap companies were involved in price rigging. Sebi impounded Rs. 18 crores, investigated over 120 individuals including more than 50 stockbrokers and decided to prosecute 13 stockbrokers.

Sebi closed the lid on six cases of price rigging—SVA Udyog, Magan Industries, SVL Capital, Amit International, Rahul Merchandising and Adeshwar Cotton—after five months of rigorous investigations.

Of the Rs. 20 crores frozen by the Bombay Stock Exchange (BSE), Rs. 17.52 crores would be transferred into the Investor Protection Fund. The balance would be released.

Sebi would initiate suspension proceedings against the stockbrokers involved. However, in the cases of individuals, for the first time, Sebi would debar them from dealing in securities, albeit for a fixed time period. Action would be taken under the Unfair and Fraudulent Trade Practices Act.

Sebi Chairman D.R. Mehta said this was a significant move in instilling confidence into investors and cracking down on financial crimes. Sebi's Senior Executive Director (Vigilance) L.K. Singhvi said the financial penalty was likely to hit the offenders the hardest. Sebi has conclusively established that two types of modus operandi were used for price rigging.

In the first, operators used to corner large blocks of shares when the issue was open and subsequently created an oversold position in the secondary market. In the second, operators used to corner large blocks of shares in the secondary market and then create a position.

The operators used to later supply stock at auctions and make huge killings.

Sebi had uncovered the following evidence in these companies:

SVA Udyog—The company's share price shot up from Rs. 40 to Rs. 155 in a short period. Sebi investigated over 30 individuals including about 10 stockbrokers. Six stockbrokers and two individuals would be prosecuted. The prominent stockbrokers involved were N.F. Lagrana, S.J. Tiberwal and Ramkishan Sekhsaria. The individual entities were Dimple Shah and Mukut stockbroking.

Magan Industries—The share price shot up from Rs. 27 to Rs. 118 accompanied by a spectacular rise in volumes. Four brokers and 13 individuals were investigated. Two brokers have been found guilty. They included Ajay Vakharia and S.I. Agarwal.

Adeshwar Cotton—Sebi had established the involvement of Kannan Dalal, daughter of Ahmedabad-based stockbroker Devendra Kantilal Dalal or DK, as he is known in the markets. Price rigging operations in this scrip were apparently done through a front of six finance companies.

Amit International—Of the 15.5 lakh shares forming part of the capital, a whopping 14 lakh shares were cornered. The price shot up from Rs. 35 to Rs. 280. Twenty entities including four brokers, Tibrewal and Lagrana were again found guilty.

SVL Capital—The price shot up from Rs. 60 to Rs. 220. Unfortunately, for Sebi most of the positions were auctioned before the regulatory body moved in. Broker involvement could not be established but one individual, Hiren Sanghvi, has been implicated.

Rahul Merchandising—For the first time, a non-Mumbai broker was involved—K.C. Badiya from Jaipur Stock Exchange, about 20 entities including 14 brokers were grilled in this case. The price had shot up from Rs. 27 to Rs. 120.

The Warning Signals

There are plenty of subtle warnings investors can look for to protect themselves from dubious investments. A little known by heavily traded scrip should set the antennae tingling. Ask whether;

- The company was recently listed and opened trading at modest levels before climbing to new highs. Often, operators start rigging share price immediately after listing and mop up shares at low levels.
- There has been a precipitous fall in the share price, even if the share was listed at un-naturally high levels.
- Volumes have suddenly increased despite low paid up capital.
- The issue fared well in the market. If it just scraped through, the sudden spurt in volume is a sure sign of extraordinary interest.
- Another group company is planning to enter the market as well? If it is listed shares of other group companies are likely to be manipulated.

And investors should also avoid lesser known leasing and finance companies as far as possible.

When the National Stock Exchange (NSE) came into existence investors had high expectations that greater transparency and trading in a computerised environment would ease the problems they face. With its wide reach and shorter settlement periods, it promised a relief for the small and genuine investors. However, as things are today speculation is prevalent on this exchange too. For example,

NSE suspended trading in Maruti Organics for two days, *i.e.* July 10 and 11, 1996, pending investigations on allegations of widespread fraud and manipulation.

During the early part of July 1996, the exchange officials received complaints from its trading members about a group of persons putting through substantial transactions in Maruti Organics, a Hyderabad-based company, through a number of trading members to manipulate the market.

The *modus operandi* adopted was that a person would approach a trading member to transact in the security, pay up the relevant margin amounts, build confidence through small transactions and then take large positions.

On July 3 and 4, 1996 trading members reported that large buy transactions were put through and subsequently the clients absconded.

According to the exchange officials, similar operations was carried out on an organised basis across centres like Hyderabad, Madras, Mumbai, Bangalore and other exchanges with the intention to maintain the price of the said security so as to be able to unload stock.

NSE is investigating the matter. However, the exchange has decided to withhold the securities and funds paid-in towards the settlement.

The price of Maruti Organics has reportedly fallen below Rs. 15 on the Hyderabad Stock Exchange. The price hovered around Rs. 50 on the NSE. This is the third time that the exchange has suspended trading in a scrip.

Earlier, the exchange had suspended trading indefinitely in Rupangi Impex following a directive by Sebi.

With the low brokerage it becomes very easy for a speculator to operate on the NSE. For some shares, the brokerage fee is as low as 25 paise. But much worse than that is that some dealers have virtually opened a casino, where an annual membership fee is charged and a member can trade through the terminals on a daily basis, squaring off the position by the end of the day's trading. These are dens for pure speculation and clearly indicate how the systems can be misused. Here, no one is interested in taking deliveries and the traded volumes continue to be very high.

7

Mutual Funds

What are Mutual Funds

There is no universally accepted or legal definition of the term 'Mutual Fund'. It is a loose term which embraces a wide variety of investment companies. Broadly speaking, a mutual fund is an investment trust, that invests generally in stock market securities, both equity as well as debt. The pool of funds from its participants are then invested in equity, bonds, debentures and other instruments. The object is to maximise the return and minimise the risk to the investor who participates in these investments through mutual funds.

They have emerged as the chief vehicle of investment of individual savings world over. Mutual funds emerged in the US and the UK during the 1920's. In UK, nearly 80 per cent of the investors look to the mutual funds. They are called Unit Trusts. In the US an individual even with $ 1 million of investible funds takes the mutual funds route to investing in equity, instead of resorting to direct participation. This is so, even though he has access to a mass of information like Standard and Poor's estimate and Don Jones index to guide him in taking his own investment decisions.

Presently, in the US there are nearly 5,000 mutual funds schemes with assets of $ 1.8 million invested by 75 million Unit holders, a four-fold increase since 1982. By the turn of the century, the total assets are likely to touch $ 4 trillion. The largest fund, Fidelity's Magellan Fund, manages funds aggregating $ 268 billion. In the US, the mutual fund business is growing at an annual rate of 20 to 25 per cent. According to a review conducted by Goldman Sachs, a leading US merchant banker, mutual funds are now the market's driving force.

In Europe too, the trend is similar. The major stock exchange at Luxembourg which has developed specialised skills in Euroissues, had 67 mutual funds, 'Funds Commons' as they are known. In 1990, the number of funds increased to 268. In keeping with the general trend, there was a dramatic surge in the mutual funds investments and at the end of April 1993, the number of funds stood at 473 with net assets of a staggering LUF 5,27,250 billion.

Mutual funds made their entry in India in 1964 with the Unit Scheme 64 launched by the Unit Trust of India (UTI). UTI was set up under the UTI Act, 1963, to operate both as a financial institution and an investment trust. Unit Scheme 64 turned out to be extremely popular, initially as a vehicle for domestic savings, subsequently as an instrument of corporate holding as well.

It is only during the last five years that the liberalised economy and industrial policies brought a boom in individual corporate investment. With the rising inflation and the reduction in the rates of interest on company deposits and bank deposits there was a switch over to corporate investment. The common investor redirected his efforts to increase his prosperity by participating in the capital market activities. The financial institutions and banks in the public sector entered into corporate investment business in the background of their expertise in merchant banking and financial lending business. Gradually, private sector and joint sector sponsors have also forayed into this area of operation. There has been a sudden increase in the number of mutual funds operating in this country.

Organisation of Mutual Funds

There are now 32 mutual funds and 258 schemes, handling around Rs. 80,000 crores. The UTI alone handles about Rs. 60,000 crores with 49 schemes. The names of the funds are as follows:

1. BOI Mutual Fund
2. Canbank Mutual Fund
3. Indbank Mutual Fund
4. PNB Mutual Fund
5. SBI Mutual Fund
6. Bank of Baroda Mutual Fund
7. Unit Trust of India
8. LIC Mutual Fund
9. GIC Mutual Fund
10. ICICI Mutual Fund
11. IDBI Mutual Fund
12. Kothari Pioneer Mutual Fund (First Private Sector Mutual fund started in November 1993)

13. Morgan Stanley Mutual Fund
14. Jardine Flemming Mutual Fund
15. H.B. Mutual Fund
16. J.M. Mutual Fund
17. Reliance Mutual Fund
18. Alliane Capital Mutual Fund
19. Birla Mutual Fund
20. Tata Mutual Fund
21. Shriram Mutual Fund
22. Apple Mutual Fund
23. 20 Century Mutual Fund
24. Taurus Mutual Fund
25. Centurion Mutual Fund
26. ITC Threadneedle Mutual Fund
27. DSP Merrill Lynch Fund
28. CRB Mutual Fund
29. Anagram—Wellington
30. Sundaram Newton Mutual Fund
31. Cholamandalam—Cazenore
32. First India Mutual Fund

Types of Mutual Funds

There are different types of mutual funds. Typically, they can be classified either on the basis of their capital structure, *i.e.* open-end or closed-end funds, or according to their financial objectives, *i.e.* growth funds, income funds and savings funds, etc.

A Closed-end mutual fund: is an investment company which has a fixed number of units, unless subsequently enhanced through rights and bonus issues, which are openly traded on the stock market after their initial public issue or offer a continuous repurchase. You can enter the fund either at the outset when its shares are offered for subscription to the public, or later by buying its units through your stockbroker in the open market, if the fund is listed.

Open-End fund: On the other hand, in an open-end fund, the number of units is not fixed at the outset. It varies from day-to-day as investors enter or leave the fund. You can buy units in an open-end mutual fund directly from the concerned investment company on any day at its announced purchase price. Similarly, you are allowed to leave the fund at any time you like by selling your units back to the company at its declared re-purchase price. The resale and re-purchase price is generally fixed at, or around, the net asset value (NAV) of the units. The units of an open-end fund are generally not listed or quoted on the stock markets. As an investor in an open-end mutual fund one deals directly with the investment company and need not approach one's stockbroker for purchase or sale of its shares. However, certain open-end fund like UTI-64 can also be traded through OTCEI.

UTI's Mastershares, Mastergain, Mastergrowth; Morgan Stanley's Growth Fund, CRB's Arihand Mangal, Canbank Mutual's Canstar, Taurus The Newshare, Apples Midas Fund, SBIs Magnum Global Fund 1994, LIC Mutual Fund Dhanavarsha series are typical examples of closed-end mutual funds, whereas Unit-64 scheme of the Unit Trust of India, Centurion's Open Fund, Apple's Mutual Fund, JM's Equity Liquid, Balanced & GIC's Fortune 94 are open-ended mutual funds.

From the point of view of their financial objectives, Indian mutual funds can be divided into four categories: growth funds, income funds, income-cum-growth funds and tax planning funds. Growth funds normally invest a large portion of their funds (generally over 70 per cent) in equity, whereas income funds do the exact reverse by investing over 70 per cent of their funds in debentures and bonds. Income-cum-growth funds try to strike a balance between growth and income by allocating their funds almost equally between equity and debentures. Tax planning funds fall into a different category because investments in them are eligible for a tax rebate of 20 per cent under section 88 of the Income-Tax Act. As far as their financial objectives are concerned, they can be either growth funds or income funds or a mix of both.

Advantages

Investing in mutual funds has three major advantages:

(i) When you invest in mutual fund you are entrusting your money to full-time professional money-managers who make all the investment decisions on your behalf. This is a major advantage for small investors who lack sufficient knowledge and experience to launch out on their own and also cannot afford or do not have access to high-calibre and expensive investment advisors or services. Also, mutual funds are a convenient investment media for investors who do not have the temperament or the time for exacting homework required to watch over and manage a well-diversified portfolio. Successful stock market investment requires a cool head and emotional detachment. This objective can be achieved by entrusting funds to professional managements.

(ii) Mutual funds enables to get the full benefit of diversification which one may not be able to get when he is investing small sums of money on his own. The minimum amount required to build a reasonably diversified portfolio would be around Rs. one lakh. A mutual fund like UTI's Master-shares enables to get the benefits of a diversified portfolio spread over a 100 companies belonging to diverse industry groups with an investment which can be as low as Rs. 3,000. If one manages his own investments then it may take as long as six months or even one year to build a large and well-diversified portfolio. By investing in a mutual fund, on the other hand, one gets the benefit of instant diversification by placing only one buy order with stockbroker.

(iii) By virtue of their large asset base and shareholder population, the mutual funds enjoy greater liquidity than most company shares. Open-end funds are generally more liquid than closed-end funds. If one has investible funds which he may require at short notice then mutual funds often offer a better and more convenient investment choice.

Disadvantages

There are basically two disadvantages of investing in mutual funds:

(i) Professional money-managers, the kinds that manage mutual funds tend to be conservative, risk-aversive and unimaginative. As a result, they generally cannot take bold, timely decisions which are quite often required for earning really big profits. Also, since they are usually under considerable pressure to produce short-term results they are less inclined to take a long-term view and thus miss out on the really big long-term gains.

(ii) Mutual funds provide the advantages of diversification but deny the advantage of concentration. In certain special situations in the stock market, an investment strategy based on concentration can give vastly superior returns than one based on diversification. Investment and trading strategies based on concentration, however, are strictly for professionals and knowledgeable investors. For beginners and in experienced investors, diversification is advisable for greater safety of returns.

Income Schemes

There are different schemes floated by the Indian mutual funds, income schemes have undoubtedly been very popular. This particular phenomenon is by no means peculiar to India alone. In the West, too, there are 'bond funds' which invest predominantly in bonds and other fixed income securities. In the US there are 'contracted schemes' that offer a minimum yield. In the Indian context, however, this aspect acquires added significance.

Till the yesteryears the average Indian was essentially a "piggy-bank" depositor. He graduated to fixed deposit schemes of nationalised banks and small savings instruments and was content to have a fixed and steady flow of income. Times have changed. The equity cult has reached far beyond the privileged few and now even common people have started joining the long queues for filing applications for primary issues.

In the UK, such regular income funds are gaining increased popularity. Many unit trust schemes have been tailored to provide monthly or quarterly returns. The Personal Equity Plans (PEPs) floated by the unit trusts provide a variety of choice to the investor. For instance, one of the funds, Guinnes Flight, has three choices for income plans:

- *Income Share Trust*: With an investment portfolio in income shares of split capital investment trusts.
- *Equity and Bond Income Trust*: With asset allocation in a balanced portfolio of UK equities and sterling bonds.
- *High Income Trust*: Investing in UK companies with strong balance sheets and where dividend yields are above The Financial Times All Shares Index.

Another fund manager, Murray Johnstone, has launched an innovative plan to pay monthly income at a level decided by the investor upto nine per cent annually—really handsome by Western standards.

Income-Cum-Growth Schemes

In India, fund managers are quite fond of terming some of their schemes as income-cum-growth. The difference is mostly semanti,: as stated earlier, most income schemes of mutual funds have provision for capital appreciation of their units.

Since the money raised by them is deployed not only in fixed income securities to provide for a steady flow of income but also in equities. Instances of such schemes are Kothari/Pioneer Prima Fund, SBI Mutual Funds Magnum Triple 91, GIC Mutual Fund's Balanced Fund, Ind Prakash of Indian Bank Mutual Fund, etc. Many of these are listed on stock exchanges and their quotations reflect the appreciation, or otherwise, in their units.

Unit Scheme 64

Unit Scheme 64 launched by the Unit Trust of India (UTI) in 1964 is the premier and the oldest mutual fund scheme in India, and undoubtedly the most popular. It is an open-ended fund. Sales and repurchases are typically allowed throughout the year except during the month of June every year when the books are closed. During January to June 1995, however, the sale of units was suspended.

The sale price of units is fixed by UTI in July every year use to remain valid for one month after which the price was revised. But more even in July the price is charged after 10/15 days. Along with the sale price, the repurchase price is also fixed. The latter is lower than the sale price, the spread being of the order of 6.5 per cent to 7 per cent. When the scheme was initially launched the sale price was fixed at par, *i.e.* Rs. 10. Subsequently it was increased to include the element of dividend declared for the previous year.

A person who holds the units at the time of book closing is entitled to the full year dividend declared for that year. Irrespective of date of purchase of units he also has the option to join the re-investment plan in which the dividend is re-invested in his account by adding the number of units purchased at the price prevailing in July. Since the minimum prescribed lot is of 100 units (recently raised from 50 units) the difference in the amount is refunded to the investor. In June 1992, UTI declared a dividend of 25 per cent on Unit 64, next year it was raised to 26 per cent. The effective yield on the units had declined from 17.87 per cent to 17.45 per cent. The investors, however, were shocked when on June 23, 1994 the dividend of 26 per cent was maintained, the effective yield had declined to 16.25 per cent. For those who bought these units during the year 1993-94, this represented a case of diminishing returns for the first time in the history of this scheme.

History was repeated in 1995 when the dividend was maintained at 26 per cent but its effective yield declined to 15.76 per cent because of issue of bonus shares. Unit-holders have benefitted by right shares below its sales price by UTI.

There are certain special features of the Unit Scheme 64. Initially, partial repurchase was not permitted. It is now allowed. There was no provision for transfer of these units. Now, it is permissible. It also implies that one does not necessarily have to get all the units repurchased officially if one needs money. This can be done by sale in the market through 'transfer'. The transfer prices are generally lower than the sale price and higher than the repurchase price.

This scheme was essentially designed as a vehicle for domestic investment. In subsequent years it also became an instrument for corporate holding. Banks, non-banking financial companies, even manufacturing companies invest in units in order to get substantial returns.

In 1986-87, the unit capital of this scheme was Rs. 149 crores. The corporates, however, found it most lucrative to park their funds in the Unit Scheme 64, mainly due to the concessions offered under section 80M of the Income Tax Act. The unit capital grew to Rs. 859 crores in 1987-88, Rs. 2,322 crores in 1988-89 and further rose to Rs. 3,201 crores in 1989-90. As discussed earlier, hectic trading in these units in the secondary market lead to units being purchased even as high as Rs. 17.80 in November 1991. As a result, active market players in these units were reported to have incurred losses running into crores of rupees.

In 1995, the share of corporates declined from 89 per cent in 1988 to nearly 68 per cent.

Handsome tax benefits had been granted to the corporates. Under section 80M of the Income Tax Act, returns from units were totally exempt from tax because the government wanted to promote the venture. Once it came of age, the concessions were withdrawn in a phased manner; from 100 per cent exemption to 80 per cent in 1992-93 and 40 per cent in 1993-94 to provide a 'level playing field' to other mutual funds.

To collect more funds from Unit Scheme 64 subscribers UTI hit upon a novel scheme in 1990. Unit-holders were offered the opportunity to invest in an equity growth scheme Unit Scheme 2000 (UGS 2000), the second growth scheme launched by UTI—upto a ceiling of 200 units. The response was predictably favourable and the fund was able to raise Rs. 193.91 crores in the scheme.

This was repeated in 1991 when the same offer was made for the next close-ended growth scheme, Unit scheme 5000 (UGS 5000).

Unit Scheme 64—Assessment

The Unit Scheme 64 gave lower returns to the investors because UTI, with its financial clout, began to aid sick industries and subscribe to new issues, many of which failed to take off. The high corpus in this scheme was sought to be utilised in inter-scheme transfers to support and sustain the health of its other schemes.

The main cause of concern for the investor was that the incidence of loans to companies and public sector under-takings, including the Indian Railways, advanced by UTI from these funds. In June 1993, the figure rose to Rs. 1,713.94 crores (16.4 per cent of corpus) from Rs. 1,097.29 crores in 1992 (12.7 per cent of corpus). The unrealised debt element of the scheme stood at a staggering Rs. 5,000 crores. Then there was the questionable private placement of Rs. 942 crores in Reliance shares. The loss was reportedly booked to Unit Scheme 64. Then there was inter-scheme transfers and discrepancies which if not reconciled but finally determined, and admitted to be 'adjusted to the accounts of Unit Scheme 1964'. This is a serious matter since unit-holders of this scheme cannot be made to subsidise losses incurred by the trust in other schemes.

Features such as these which surfaced during 1993 and 1994 affected the scheme's credibility adversely. Nevertheless Unit Scheme 64 remains the most important and popular instrument.

In addition to Unit Scheme 64, there are income schemes of other mutual funds. SBI Mutual Funds has its Magnum Regular Income Scheme in which dividends are declared annually and sale and repurchase prices are fixed every month as in the case of Unit 64. Life Insurance Corporation of India Mutual Fund (LIC MF) has a number of schemes that offer annual dividends. Some of the mutual funds prefer to call their schemes 'income-cum-growth' though as stated earlier some capital appreciation of mutual fund units is always implied even when regular dividends are declared.

Income Schemes

Income Schemes provide no hedge against inflation. Mutual funds are getting increasingly seized of the investor's preference for a fund which takes care of inflationary trends. SBI Mutual Fund, therefore, launched its Rising Monthly Income Scheme during the later part of 1993 to provide dividends on a rising scale in the hope of substantial capital appreciation of its units. It was also proposed to list the scheme on the stock exchanges. During its duration of seven years (extendable to eight years at the discretion of the trustees) there is no provision for repurchase—the essential safety net in all such schemes.

Another popular instrument of savings, particularly for retired people, are monthly income schemes in which investors put a sizeable portion of their post-retirement benefits to get a steady flow of monthly income to supplement their modest pension. UTI was the pioneer in launching such schemes, followed by SBI Mutual Fund. In 1990, Bank of India Mutual Fund (BOIMF) launched the Rising Monthly Income Scheme to provide dividends on an ascending scale year by year.

With the ban imposed by Sebi on mutual funds promising any pre-determined rates of return, no such schemes were launched after 1991 by any mutual fund till 1996 except UTI which is outside the regulatory control of Sebi. Mutual funds have been allowed to assure returns once again. Provided AMCs and the trusts stand as guarantors.

Growth Schemes

Mutual fund schemes designed primarily to achieve capital appreciation of units rather than regular yield through dividends are commonly known as growth schemes. The term is a misnomer since, as already explained earlier, mutual funds deploy their assets not only in debt instruments like debentures, bonds and other fixed income securities but also in equities, the value of which rises and falls in the market. In the case of growth schemes, the stress is on investment in equities with high growth potential. However, income by way of dividends cannot be ruled out.

Characteristics of Growth Schemes

1. These schemes can be both close-ended as well as open-ended.
2. Their duration usually ranges from 5 to 7 years. In some cases there is stipulation that the scheme can be extended by another year at the discretion of the board of trustees. Of course, there are exceptions, Kothari-Pioneer Blue Chip Fund floated in November 1993 announced a 3-year redemption period. On the other hand, Morgan Stanley Growth Fund stipulated a duration of 15 years.
3. The schemes are usually listed on one or more major stock exchanges of India. The objective is to provide liquidity to investors.
4. In addition, there is provision in some of the schemes for mid-term repurchase from individual investors. Repurchase prices are announced by the mutual fund based on the net asset value (NAV) of the scheme after deduction of a service charge ranging from 5 per cent to 7 per cent, or even higher in certain schemes.
5. On expiry of the scheme, its units are redeemed at a price based on NAV minus service charges. Investors, however, usually have the option of investing these proceeds in another scheme of the same fund.
6. Dividends may or may not be declared annually in such schemes.
7. Rights and bonus issues may be offered from time to time.
8. NAV is published at periodic intervals ranging from a week to a month in a few cases, even quarterly.
9. Units of such schemes are accepted by banks as collateral security for loans once they are listed and actively traded—with 50 per cent margin.

One of the claims of mutual funds is that dividends attract higher tax rates than long-term capital gains arising out of appreciation of units should be taken with a pinch of salt. It is the duty of a fund manager to maximise the return to the investor and not to act as his tax consultant.

A glaring example is *Dhanvikas* (I) launched by LIC Mutual Fund in March 1993 as a 'pure' growth scheme. It was listed on the Bombay Stock Exchange on October 22, 1993 but there was practically no trading till almost mid-February 1994. Even then it was thinly traded: one of the most inactive mutual fund shares which stagnated at Rs. 8.50 in August 1994. The Units were a millstone around the investor's neck. The higher NAV of Rs. 14.43 was of no consequence to him till these were eventually repurchased.

In 1986, the first mutual fund growth scheme, Master Share was launched by UTI with a redemption period of 7 years. The scheme collected Rs. 155 crores. The issue was a major success. In 1989, UTI issued rights share at the ratio of 1 : 2 per unit and raised another Rs. 90 crores.

This was successfully listed and traded in the stock exchanges. Encouraged by this venture, other players emerged. In 1987, State Bank of India Mutual Fund (SBIMF) and Canara Bank Mutual Fund (Canbank MF) started their operations, followed by the mutual funds sponsored by the Bank of India, Indian Bank and the Punjab National Bank. Not to lag behind, Life Insurance Corporation of India (LIC) and the General Insurance Corporation of India (GIC), too, sponsored their respective mutual fund schemes.

UTI was followed by seven institutions in the public sector—five banks and two insurance companies. They all had the inherent advantage of the basic infrastructure, an overflow of funds and customer service outlets. By the end of March 1993, the total corpus of the 'Big Eight' was approximately Rs. 50,000 crores with UTI alone accounting for Rs. 40,000 crores.

The sudden surge came in 1992-93 when the total number of investors increased from 18 million to 32 million and the combined corpus rose to Rs. 38,000 crores. Much of it was accounted for by UTI Master Gain 92 which netted Rs. 4,792 crores winning for itself a place in the Guinness Book of Records but it proved a very disappointing investment with fall in price much below face value as well as dividend for years. This increase has to be viewed against the background of net assets of measly Rs. 4,000 crores in 1987 for all eight funds put together.

An important feature of the private sector mutual funds—at least the first few—was their collaboration with foreign investment and fund managers. Thus, Kothari tied up with Pioneer, the oldest fund in the US managing $ 8 billion, 20th Century with Kemper Corporation which claimed to be eighth largest fund manager in the US, managing assets worth over $ 70 billion. Credit Capital Asset Managers Inc. that launched the Taurus, Starshare had for its partners, apart from Commonwealth Development Corporation, London and Asian Development Bank, Manila, International Finance Corporation, Washington, Edinburgh Fund Manager, UK, European Commission, Brussels and Lazard Ferr and Co., New York. Lazard managed funds of $ 40 billion world-wide.

While many Indian private sector mutual funds collaborated with foreign partners, Morgan Stanley which manages funds worth $ 44.2 billion chose to go it alone. Its issue was a runaway success but so far performance is very poor.

The vital aspect of a strong research capability of foreign collaborators had been recognised and the public sector GIC Mutual Fund too reacted to the winds of change and tied with the US Soros Fund Management headed by the legendary George Soros, who manages funds worth $ 10 billion.

ICICI Mutual Funds had no overseas partner but JP Morgan provided the necessary training facilities to its personnel.

SBIMF's *Magnum Multiplier 90*

The scheme which eventually turned out to be the one most fancied by the investors was the Magnum Multiplier launched by State Bank of India Mutual Fund in November 1990. A unique feature of the scheme was the advance despatch of warrants to be converted into rights issue at par in February 1994 in the ratio of 1 : 5. The scheme netted Rs. 145 crores.

During the dizzy peak of early 1992, prices of these units were quoted as high as Rs. 120 and above. There was no obvious rationale behind such quotations but throughout 1993 and in early 1994 this was the only scrip out of 26-odd mutual fund schemes listed at the various stock exchanges which quoted at a premium to its NAV. In the second year, dividend at the rate of 18 per cent was declared. In December 1991, UTI floated

Master-plus 91 which garnered Rs. 990 crores. The units were traded at a very heavy premium in the grey markets. This was followed by the record mega issue of Mastergain 92 by UTI in April 1992. The corpus was Rs. 4,791.79 crores thus winning a place in the Guinness Book of Records.

The Life Insurance Corporation of India Mutual Fund (LICMF) has been operating a number of income schemes since 1989. They have been performing reasonably—if not in a spectacular manner. Early in 1993 it floated its 'pure' growth scheme Dhanvikas (I). The judicious investment mix and the infrastructure of LIC MF with its country-wide network of agents, elicited warm response from investors. However, the scheme was a non-starter. Undeterred, the mutual fund launched another 'pure' growth scheme—Dhansamriddhi II in July 1994 as if to prove its credentials without any proven track record to manage growth schemes.

By 1995, realisation had suddenly dawned on Indian fund managers that open-ended schemes would provide the ideal answer to the malaise that afflicted the funds' performance. This caused a near glut in the market with fund managers vying with one another in bringing about what they euphemistically term innovative features in investor service.

It is startling that the mutual funds should have taken all that long in appreciating the obvious: the advantages to the investor in having easy entry and—what is more important to him—easier exit route far outweigh the benefits of long-term growth. The fact is of vital relevance since the average 'risk-averse' Indian investor has been baptised to the equity cult—through proxy by the mutual funds—but recently having outgrown the piggy bank depositor's mentality. That his needs should have been ignored so long hardly paints the fund managers in a favourable light.

Equity Linked Savings Schemes

The equity-linked savings schemes (ELSS) popularly known as tax-planning schemes are floated by almost all the public sector mutual funds every year during the last quarter of the financial year that is during January to March.

Previously there was provision under the old section 80 CCB of the Income Tax Act which provided 100 per cent relief in income tax for investing in new issues of companies upto a ceiling of Rs. 20,000. This section has now been abolished and its essential features merged with tax benefit limited to 20 per cent of investment. Investments in approved instruments, like life insurance policies, provident fund contribution, deposits in Public Provident Fund Scheme, National Savings Scheme 92 and the National Savings Certificates of the National Savings Organisation (NSO) qualify for tax relief upto 20 per cent subject to an overall ceiling of Rs. 60,000. For writers, artists, authors, playwrights, etc. the ceiling is Rs. 70,000 and the extent of tax relief 25 per cent.

Investment upto a maximum of Rs. 10,000 in the tax-planning schemes of mutual funds qualifies for tax relief of 20 per cent, *i.e.* Rs. 2,000 (Rs. 2,500 in the cases of artists, authors, writers, dramatists, etc.) within the overall ceiling of Rs. 60,000 (Rs. 70,000 for writers, dramatists, etc.). The tax liability is thus reduced by Rs. 2,000 or Rs. 2,500 in the latter category.

These schemes are aggressively advertised by the respective mutual funds leading to their popularity, since apart from saving, they provide capital appreciation too. Some of the funds, like GIC MF and LIC MF also provide life and accident insurance cover. Investors, however, should not be taken in by these additional factors since they alone cannot be decisive, and such value addition is a dent on the investible funds of the schemes.

Detailed guidelines were issued by the government in 1992 for the pattern of investment to be followed by these schemes. Funds raised through such schemes are required to be invested in equity, convertible and preference shares, debentures, bonds, warrants and other money market instruments. In addition, 0.25 per cent of the funds collected in each scheme are to be set aside for the Development Reserve Fund to which 0.5 per cent of the net asset value (NAV) is also required to be credited. This enables both capital appreciation and higher returns to the investor.

Characteristics

The main characteristics of these schemes are:

1. The minimum investment is Rs. 500—as against Rs. 1,000 generally in other schemes. Thus a small investor can

participate in equity with as small an amount as Rs. 500, and also save on taxes in the process.

2. There is no ceiling on the upper limit of investment, but tax relief is available only upto an investment of Rs. 10,000 each year.
3. The schemes are essentially growth-oriented and aim at capital appreciation of units.
4. The duration of the schemes is generally 10 years after which the units can be redeemed on NAV-based prices with 20 per cent tax deduction at source.
5. There is a minimum lock-in period of 3 years during which the units cannot be pledged, traded or transferred. They also cannot be traded as collateral security against loans by the nationalised banks.
6. After 3 years they are generally listed at the stock exchanges where they can be traded.
7. There is provision for repurchase after 3 years by the mutual funds at a price fixed on the basis of NAV minus service charges. In addition, there is provision for tax deduction of 20 per cent at source in terms of section 194F of the Income Tax Act.

LIC MF's Dhanraksha and Dhanvridhi

LIC Mutual Fund launched a scheme, Dhanraksha 89, similar to ULIP, with separate maturity periods of 10 and 15 years. The scheme has better liquidity since the units can be encashed after a 3-year lock-in period. In addition, the concept of capital units as different from dividend units was introduced; the former represent those which are issued in lieu of the contribution paid yearly or half-yearly, whereas the latter are units issued in lieu of dividends.

LIC Mutual Fund's Dhanvridhi issued in 1989 is yet another scheme combining the various benefits of liquidity, regular returns and, more important, a higher life insurance cover. Significantly, these units are eligible as security against loans from nationalised banks. Obviously with the experience of the earlier schemes before them, mutual funds have constantly been effecting improvements.

LIC Mutual Fund launched on open-ended scheme, Dhanvidya, in November 1991 with a lock-in period of 3 years for providing scholarships to children below 18 years on annual or half-yearly basis. The minimum investment is 300 units and the maximum 10,000 units of the face value of Rs. 10 each. Besides the scholarship, free insurance cover to the child is provided by the mutual fund. The units can be encashed on maturity or even earlier with bonus, if any.

Children's Gift Growth Plan 1986

This scheme was floated by UTI in 1986 as an improved version of its earlier Children's Gift Plan. The amount can be gifted in favour of a child below of the age of 15 by any adult—parent, relative, friend, a corporate body, even a registered society, eligible trust or a guardian appointed by the court. This amount is exempted from gift tax.

Mutual Funds--An Assessment

A mutual fund's foremost duty is towards its investors. Mutual funds are primarily meant for the small investors who neither have an aptitude nor the professional background to operate in the stock market. Next to safety what the investor values most is liquidity. He should get a fair price for his investment whenever he desires instead of waiting till the termination of a scheme.

This can be possible only when the units are repurchased by the mutual fund itself or investor is able to sell them in the market once they are listed. He also justifiably expects that for meeting short-term commitments he should be able to get loans from the banks and other recognised institutions by pledging the units. At no point it should become a millstone around his neck.

Finally, the returns. This includes not just yield by way of annual dividends, but also capital appreciation of units over a period of time, apart from rights and bonus issues declared from time to time.

The norms prescribed by Sebi are undoubtedly well-intentioned. In keeping with the interests of the investors they seek to provide for a diversified portfolio and also seek to prohibit mutual funds from any undue tilt in favour of a particular industry or company.

Way back in the fifties the late Justice M.C. Chagla, while enquiring into the LIC—Mundhra deal, had stressed the paramount importance of the LIC restricting its investment to blue chip companies—that is companies with a proven track record and whose shares are actively traded in the share market and enjoy a high investment status. The same principle holds good even today in the case of mutual funds. But today the perceptions have changed.

There is another aspect of the problem. The mutual funds play a key role in the stock market activity. By virtue of sheer size of transactions, their buying and selling goes to determine the market trends.

There have been cases when the mutual funds helped ailing industries at the investor's expense. UTI purchased the unsubscribed portion of many new issues at a discounted price. Some of these issues later failed to take off. Then there was the controversy in 1993 when UTI came to the aid of Ballarpur Paper Mills, but refused to do so for the mega issue of Chambal Fertilisers which led to its devolvement. Such decisions may deem to be taken in the best interest of the investors. But it has not always been the case.

In 1991, UTI unloaded a sizeable chunk of Usha Beltron shares at a time when the jelly-filled cable industry was just picking up, and the shares were in great demand in the market.

Since Sebi's writ did not extend to UTI, the latter has been ignoring the 5 per cent ceiling (now raised to 10 per cent) as was evident from the publications of the portfolios of eight of its schemes. Apart from the blue chip companies some of the public sector undertakings, like Mahanagar Telephone Nigam Ltd., Bharat Petroleum Ltd., Bharat Heavy Electrical Ltd., featured prominently in the portfolios.

Recently, UTI investment pattern showed that it has invested Rs. 3,000 crores each in Reliance, Essar, Birlas and Tatas shares alone. Reliance shares got a drubbing in the market because of the loss of Reliance credibility as it was involved in issuing lakhs of duplicate shares.

In all developed countries there is a ceiling on a mutual fund investing in a single company. In the US and Japan it is 10 per cent of the total stocks of a company. In the UK if a fund invests more than 5 per cent in a stock of a company, it has to disclose this fact in the prospectus. Apart from the investor's interests, the regulatory body has to guard against takeover bids.

In the UK, many funds own more than five per cent of holdings but they have to disclose the complete portfolio details to the investor. The Saver and Prosper, one of the oldest unit trust runs UK Growth Fund with 5.4 per cent of its corpus invested in Glaxo,. 5 per cent in Shell Transport and Trading, 4.9 per cent in Yorkshire Electricity, 4.5 per cent in British Telecommunications, besides other concerns. It is the adequacy of disclosure norms, that gives the desired level of investor protection.

The Mutual Fund industry in India is really a late 80's phenomena. Prior to that the scene was dominated by the Unit Trust of India, which even today is the biggest player. The only other players were the Life Insurance and the General Insurance companies, which were passive risk takers. The resource base for these organisations was not related to the health of the capital market.

For example, UTI because of the tax-free dividends and the repurchase facility, became the perfect money market instrument to park corporate liquidity. Most of the individuals and corporations who invested in UTI had no clues as to how its investments were performing, nor did they care. It was after all liquid and government-owned.

The position of the insurance major was even simpler. The premiums flowed in whether the investments earned income or not. Also, the investment business was not significant enough for these giants to really worry. So, strangely enough till a few years ago, the mutual fund industry was not affected by the vagaries of the market.

All this changed dramatically when this sector was opened to the private sector. There was a rush of funds entering the market. While some were owned and managed by the State-owned banks like the State Bank of India, Bank of India, Indian Bank, Canara Bank, there were others which were promoted by professionally-owned finance companies.

All of them got off to a rousing start as share hungry small investors thronged the bourses to get a piece of the bull run. For a while, in the early 90's it looked as if the mutual funds were the final word on accessing the bourses. In 1992 the mutual funds collected Rs. 11,000 crores in the wake of stock market boom.

Unfortunately, the present situation is dismal. The last year-and-a-half (1995-96) has seen the mutual fund industry struggling, not only to get new investors into the fold, but also to retain old ones because large number of schemes NAV is below par.

These funds have not given a good return to investors. Most of them have not even given 18 per cent return which one gets from corporate deposits, actually in many cases there is negative return. Secondly, their prices on the bourses are at a substantial discounts to net asset values indicating a terrible erosion in investors confidence.

To get over this crises, a common strategy adopted by the funds was to roll over schemes due for redemption. Another significant plot experimented recently was to turn the scheme into an open-ended one.

There are a number of schemes in the former category, but the second type has limited examples. What has been the performance of these rolled over schemes? Have investors gained by continuing with the scheme or have they lost out? Let us go over the schemes to make an assessment.

The first scheme to be rolled over was the SBI Magnum Monthly Income Scheme '89 which was due for redemption in March, 1993. The scheme's original corpus was Rs. 140 crores, but a roll-over saw that go down to about half that level.

The redemption price for those who opted out of the scheme then was Rs. 103 per unit of Rs. 100. The net asset value of the scheme now hovers around Rs. 78 per unit. This is so because the scheme offered for a dividend payment of 15 per cent in the post-redemption period as against 12 per cent offered earlier. But the fund was unable to generate that kind of return on its investments and so the payouts had to be made out of its capital base, an obvious case of mis-match between the expected and the actual returns from the investments made by the fund managers.

Fortunately for investors, as the redemption is assured at the face value, that is Rs. 100, there is not much cause for worry whatever be the net asset value. But the redemption would definitely put a load on the SBI funds management, the asset management company for SBI Mutual Fund. With a unit base of about Rs. 72 crores, as of 31st March 1996, the shortfall between the actual net asset value and the redemption price would cost SBIMF nearly Rs. 16 crores.

A look at the results for the year ended 31st March 1996 shows that the SBI's scheme, MMIS, had an aggregate income of Rs. 8.8 crores and Rs. 7.1 crores of this was from dividends and interests. The rest was from profit on sale of investments. Expenses and losses on investment sold or transferred to other schemes amounted to Rs. 11.30 crores, deficit of Rs. 2.5 crores as a result. In addition, the fund needed at least Rs. 10.5 crores to make its payout of 15 per cent. The shortfall had to be taken from the corpus, resulting in a below par net asset value.

MMIS '89, however, is not an isolated case. Except for a couple of funds, all rollovers have been disastrous. For instance, Canbank Mutual Fund's Canstock was to be redeemed at Rs. 154.29 on January 31, 1995. It has, however, rolled over on February 1, 1995 for a period of five years. However, with a current net asset value of Rs. 54 investors who stayed with the scheme are worth a third of what they were almost two years ago.

For a period ending March 31, 1996, the total income was Rs. 6.11 crores as against Rs. 51.12 crores in the previous year. Expenses, losses and provisions, on the other hand, were Rs. 14.26 crores and Rs. 16.54 crores, respectively, resulting in a deficit of Rs. 8.15 crores. The fund had to skip dividend. Candouble, the Canbank Mutual Fund's other scheme, which was rolled over on February 15, 1995, for five years has a current net asset value of Rs. 19 against Rs. 22.44 at the time of redemption. Candouble's profit and loss is quite like Canstock's. The year 1995-96 witnessed a sharp decline in income to Rs. 0.93 crore from Rs. 5.99 crores in the previous year. But expenses, losses and provisioning mounted to Rs. 43.36 crores as against Rs. 38.59 crores earlier, resulting in a net deficit of Rs. 19.64 crores.

RMI-60 of Bank of India Mutual Fund faces the same problem. It was to be redeemed on August 1995, but offered a rollover. The pre-rollover unit capital of the scheme was Rs. 104.62 crores. However, with only a little more than half of the unit capital being rolled over, the post-rollover corpus stood at Rs. 54.35 crores. The net asset value was Rs. 221 at the time of redemption under the growth option and Rs. 93 now.

A look at the pre and post-rollover profile of the assets in this case shows a drastic shift, which was probably also responsible to an extent for the poor performance of the scheme in the post-rollover period. Fixed income securities and instruments, such as, deposits, debentures, and cash and bank balances constituted 51 per cent of the total assets on March 31, 1995, but declined to 42 per cent a year later. Obviously, the residual portfolio of the rolled-over unit capital had a risk profile very different from the one that existed earlier.

And even among the equity portfolio, the fund managers did not have much choice but to sell off some of the more liquid scrips to meet the redemption requirements. These liquid scrips were definitely the better ones of the portfolio. As a result, whatever was left in the portfolio was either illiquid or not of much worth.

On December 31, 1996, the MMIS will be due for redemption. But if the scenario continues to remain the same the fund managers will find it difficult to sell off these scrips.

But there is the other side to the coin. There are schemes which have managed to perform well after the rollover. Some of these are the Indbank Scheme Swarna Pushpa, which has seen its net asset value rise to Rs. 109.94 from Rs. 101.72. Some of the LIC's Mutual Fund's Dhanvarsha series schemes have also managed to hold fort.

Master Share, the second scheme to be rolled after MMIS '89 has also just about managed to maintain its worth. In November 1993, when the scheme was up for redemption, its net asset value was Rs. 49.70 per unit. Thereafter, the scheme offered its unit holders a 1:3 bonus and a 1:1 rights in 1993-94 followed by another 1:5 bonus in 1994-95. The current net asset value of the scheme at Rs. 21.36 per unit shows that it has just about been able to maintain its position. However, as the scheme does not provide any exit options, the returns ought to be measured against the market price which is at 40 per cent plus a discount to the market.

The fund managers have their own logic for adopting rollovers. They contend that the rollovers have several advantages. The cost of winding up a scheme and then floating a new one is ultimately borne by the investor. Rollovers attempt to save on such costs. Also, when a scheme is wound up, there are costs associated in selling the portfolio, sending payments to unit-holders, and loss of interest when the cheques are in transit. The time lag until the money is reinvested would also be costly. Then the transaction costs in building the portfolio again.

Fund managers insist that if a big scheme sold off a large portfolio, there would be a crash in prices, while large buying could push up the prices.

Normally, an investor would favour redemption. But sometimes the rollovers may not be bad provided there is more openness and transparency on the part of the fund managers.

Most of these mutual funds have a poor track record as far as transparency and investor communication is concerned. They assume that by virtue of their being public sector organisations, they do not need to disclose the details of their operations. In fact, a mutual fund before asking an investor whether he would like to rollover or redeem, should try to ensure that he knows what the total portfolio of the scheme is.

It is only after a look at the portfolio that an investor would be able to get an idea about the quality of the fund's assets and whether he should opt for redemption or a rollover.

It is also important for the investor to know the fund manager's strategy in selling stocks to meet the redemption requests. After all, it is the remaining portfolio which should determine the future performance of the scheme.

UTI, as discussed earlier, does not have a very good track record on these matters, but it seems to be improving on this front. The full disclosure of the portfolio under its Grand-Master and Master Gain schemes, which have become open-ended ones, are a step in the right direction. The fund manager was very clear about the class of scrips that would be off-loaded to meet the redemption and repurchase requests. In these two cases, the fund managers had their strategy chalked out before going to the public. The investor knew what the quality of the assets would be and where his fund was going to be invested.

Every investor knows that a change in the characteristics of the portfolio has a bearing on its future performance. The change could be by way of a shift in the asset allocation pattern or a reshuffle in the equity holding. However, in tune with the changing market scenario, fund managers may have to change their investment mix and strategy. It is, therefore, important that funds make it a policy to declare their portfolios on a regular basis.

The apprehensions of investors are particularly grave considering the failure of some funds to honour commitments. The latest being the PNB Mutual Fund, which has suspended its repurchase of PNB Premium Plus. PNBMF had promised to repurchase the units at face value. But the slide in the NAV of the scheme has been much more than anticipated by the fund. This, coupled with the repurchase request from large investors, has forced the fund to suspend repurchase. This is the third fund, after Canstar and the GIC Big Value, to go back on its commitments.

Yet, funds still believe that promises and assurances are the only way to attract investors. Although not many dare to offer a scheme in the current market, there are those who come out with some kind of income schemes, giving the impression that returns are assured. Sebi does not allow funds to make promises. So different names like 'targeted returns' are being given. These targets and promises have to be revised every year.

For instance, UTI's monthly income plan 96-IV has a 15 per cent minimum targeted dividend. But the prospectus says that if the actual income falls below the target then unit-holders may suffer loss of unit capital. There are others like LIC-Dhanvarsha-9 which actually makes a commitment to investors that if there is a shortfall income for distribution at the indicated dates, the asset management company would bear the difference.

A cursory look at the working of the mutual funds reveals that while all the funds without exception have lost their values continuously during the past two years (1994-96), their respective asset management companies (AMCs) have thrived.

They have received their share of the cake, though there has been a continuous reduction in the value of the assets they have managed.

As a test case, a study of the recently published financial results of Morgan Stanley Mutual Fund (MSMF) as on March 31, 1996, reveals very interesting facts. MSMF, which was floated on January 6, 1994, with a great fanfare, collected more than Rs. 900 crores from the public. So heavy was the rush to subscribe to these units that there was a black market in forms, premium on units and even lathicharges on the investors who waited in long queues in the hot sun.

Today, the NAV of MSMF units is only 7.14 each and the market price is a mere Rs. 6.45, *i.e.* a net loss of 36 per cent to the investor over a period of two-and-a-half years. Taking into account the normal return of 18 per cent, he has actually lost 81 per cent. Cumulatively, this works out to be Rs. 729 crores on the fund base of Rs. 900 crores.

Now let us look at the benefits that have accrued to Morgan Stanley Asset Management Co. Pvt. Ltd. (MSAMC). It has received Rs. 19.75 crores as "investment management and Advisory fees" (Rs. 12.33 crores for 1994-95 and Rs. 7.42 crores for 1995-96). This at the rate of 1.25 per cent upto Rs. 100 crores and one per cent thereafter.

This represents the maximum permissible limit under present Sebi guidelines which has been charged to the fund on a weekly basis. Further, MSAMC has been reimbursed all the expenses incurred by it in the administration of the fund.

Thus, MSAMC has squeezed out every paise available to it and not found it necessary to forego voluntarily and of the benefits, though the fund has performed poorly.

When we compare the income which MSAMC has received with its paid up capital at Rs. 5 crores, this works out to a return on investment of Rs. 40 per share over a period of two years. This means that for causing a loss of Rs. 729 crores to investors the AMC has received a fee of Rs. 40 crores. The same is the case with the portfolio managers, Akash Prakash and Ashutosh Sinha. They have received fat salaries and perks (reported to be Rs. 2 lakh per month each) though their performance shows that they should be sacked.

As in the case of MSAMC, all AMCs can charge their management fee irrespective of fund's performance. Unfortunately, no penalty is built into system to discourage bad performance.

This is the basic drawback in the guidelines which has resulted in uniformly bad performance by all mutual funds. What is still tragic is that as per the current regulations, there is no guideline which compels AMCs even to reveal their financial position to the investors.

Thus, while the assets managed by AMCs are depreciating, their own assets are multiplying and this is totally hidden from public view.

The major problems responsible for this dismal performance of mutual funds lies in the failure of the fund managers in exercising commercial judgment while making investments. Small investors were under the impression that they were putting their money in expert hands. The least that the fund managers would have done was to ensure that the investors suffered the minimum loss in bearish market. Here they have failed and they lost not only money, but investor's faith.

On July 1, 1996, Sebi made sweeping changes in the mutual funds operations. The focus of the change was on the deregulations of the funds and bring in transparency in its functioning. The changes removed lot of restrictions on mutual funds.

The changes included the removal of stipulations relating to a minimum corpus funds, refund of money in the case of shortfall in mobilisation, industry exposure, relaxation of rules relating to investment in a single company, re-issue of repurchased units and permitting a hybrid of the close and open-ended funds, known as the interval funds. Investment in specialised schemes have been allowed. Simultaneously, the discretion given to fund managers to manage their portfolios has been considerably enhanced and asset management companies have been allowed to diversify their activities into the management of pension funds and venture capital funds.

Sebi's Recommendations

The following were the Sebi's recommendations to boost the Mutual Funds:

1. In a bid to eliminate the problems of discounts on listed MF Schemes, Sebi has allowed close ended schemes to be listed within six months and removed the requirement of immediate listing.
2. It has allowed mutual funds to issue repurchased units which will provide liquidity to investors and provide an incentive to MFs to repurchase units from investors in large quantities.
3. The MFs can now launch pension schemes under section 88C of the Income Tax Act on the same lines as retirement plan approved by the government for UTI.
4. The proposal to introduce derivative trading has been approved and the board has recommended amendment in the rules.
5. It has approved the NAV Committee report on standardization of valuation norms, computation of NAV, accounting practices and fee structure.
6. Listing of open-ended schemes will pave the way for listing of US-64 and ease the redemption pressure on UTI. It has also decided to do away with requirement of minimum amount for initial corpus and removed the requirements of refund.
7. The investment restrictions of MFs have also been eased. Now MF schemes can invest upto 10 per cent of paid up-capital of a single company which was five per cent earlier. The basic idea is to restrict this investment to check undue tilt in favour of a particular industry, company or corporate group and to safeguard the interest of investors.
8. The restrictions on investments in one company or one industry has been relaxed.
9. The NAV Committee norms will also apply to all schemes of UTI. The existing schemes will be getting three months for compliance.
10. The existing restrictions on fund managers on investment in money market instruments have been withdrawn. Now MFs are free to determine its portfolio composition and invest in money market instruments.

11. MFs have been allowed to borrow upto a maximum of 20 per cent of their net assets of the scheme for a maximum period of six months for the purpose of meeting redemptions. This will ease the liquidity problems for MFs at the time of redemption.
12. Sebi has laid special emphasis on trustees to ensure that there is no conflict of interest in the dealings of AMCs.
13. Approval of majority of unit-holders will be taken into confidence for any changes in the scheme. It is now obligatory to remit redemption proceeds within 10 working days from due date.
14. The asset management companies have also been allowed to diversify their activities to management of other funds like offshore funds, venture capital funds and pension funds and additional disclosure requirements have also been laid down.
15. Sebi has prohibited the use of lotteries, gifts and offering of units at a differential price to any class of shareholders. It has also laid down a code of conduct for AMCs which will ensure core business principles.

In a significant move on December 17, 1996, Sebi tightened screws on asset management companies trustees to make them totally accountable for the performance of mutual funds. Sebi will now directly interact with trustees of all AMCs, including institutions like Unit Trust of India.

This followed a major regulatory shift in stance whereby the entire onus of responsibility for mutual funds has been placed on trustees as opposed to the AMC representations. A trustee has been defined as a person who holds the property of the mutual funds in trust for the benefit of the unit-holders. Trustees have a battery of tasks to perform ranging from ensuring good conduct to filing half yearly details and taking unit-holder's consent whenever unit-holder's interests have to be protected.

Trustees also have to ensure that an AMC empanels its brokers diligently, monitor securities, transactions, not give undue or unfair advantage to any associate and even appoint auditors, compliance officers, registrars and prepare compliance manuals and internal control mechanism.

Registration of Mutual Funds

Every mutual fund shall be registered with the Sebi. An application for registration shall be made in Form A by the sponsor and shall be addressed to the Sebi. Every application for registration shall be accompanied with an application fee by means of a cheque or bank draft payable in the name of the Sebi at Bombay:

Application fees payable by Mutual Fund	Rs. 5,000
Registration fees payable by Mutual Fund	Rs. 10,00,000
Annual Fees payable by Mutual Fund	Rs. 1,00,000

The Sebi may require the sponsor to furnish such further information or clarifications as may be considered necessary for grant of registration. The sponsor or his authorised representative shall, if so required, appear before the Sebi for personal representation.

Consideration of the Application

The Sebi on the basis of information furnished in the application and after obtaining such further information, as may be required shall as soon as possible but not later than three months from the date of receipt of all information, decide on the application for registration.

For the purpose of grant of registration, the Sebi shall take into account all matters which are relevant to efficient and orderly conduct of the affairs of a mutual fund and in particular the following namely:

(a) The sponsor has a sound track record and experience in the relevant field of financial services for a minimum period of five years, professional competence, financial soundness and general reputation of fairness and integrity in all his business transactions. Sound track record shall mean net worth, dividend paying capacity and profitability of the sponsor.

(b) Mutual fund is in the form of a trust and the trust deed has been approved by the Sebi.

(c) An Asset Management Company who holds an approval of the Sebi has been appointed to manage the affairs of the mutual fund and operate the schemes of such fund.

(d) The sponsor contributes at least 40 per cent to the net worth of the Asset Management Company.

(e) The sponsor or any of its director or the principal officer to be employed by the mutual fund having the management of the affairs of the business is or has not at any time been convicted for any offence involving moral turpitude or has been found guilty of any economic offence.

Grant of Registration

The Sebi on being satisfied that the application is complete in all respects and all particulars sought have been furnished and that the mutual fund is eligible for registration may register the mutual fund subject to

(a) receipt of registration fee indicated in Schedule II in a manner specified by the Sebi.

(b) the terms and conditions specified in Regulation 12.

Where a mutual fund is found to be eligible for grant of registration the Sebi shall grant a certificate of Registration in Form B.

Terms and Conditions of Registration

The registration granted to a mutual fund shall be subject to the mutual fund fulfilling the following terms and conditions:

(a) Complying with the provisions of the Sebi Regulations.

(b) Informing forthwith the Sebi, as soon as it comes to the knowledge of the sponsor or the trustees, that any information or particulars previously submitted to the Sebi was either misleading or false in any material respect.

(c) Informing forthwith the Sebi of any material change in the information or particulars previously furnished which have a bearing on the registration granted by it.

(d) The sponsor, the asset management company, trustees and the custodian comply with the provisions of the regulations.

(e) Allowing examination of directors, officers and other employees in the course of inspection and extending full cooperation in this behalf.

(f) Agreeing to produce books of accounts, documents and such other information as sought for by the Sebi in the course of inspection.

Where an applicant does not satisfy the requirements, the Sebi shall reject the application. The decision to reject the application shall be communicated to the applicant in writing, stating therein the grounds on which the application has been rejected.

The applicant who is aggrieved by the decision of the Sebi may, within a period of thirty days from the date of receipt of such information, apply to the Sebi for reconsideration of its decision.

The Sebi shall as soon as possible in the light of the submission made in the application and wherever necessary after giving an opportunity for personal hearing convey its decision in writing to the applicant.

Every mutual fund registered shall pay annual fee for every financial year from the year following the year of registration. The annual fee shall be remitted to the Sebi by means of a cheque or bank draft payable in the name of the Sebi at Bombay.

Where a mutual fund fails to remit the annual fee the Sebi may prohibit the mutual fund from launching any new schemes till the fees has been remitted. The Sebi may on being satisfied with the reasons for the delay and subject to such conditions as it may deem fit permit the sponsor to pay the annual fee at any time within two months from the commencement of the financial year to which such fee relates.

Suspension, Cancellation

In case of default, the registration of the mutual fund may be suspended or cancelled after due inquiry as prescribed in the regulations.

Establishment of Mutual Funds

There are four parties to a mutual fund. These are: the Sponsor, the Asset Management Company (AMC), the Trustees and the Custodian. Mutual Fund is constituted in the form of a Trust in accordance with the provisions of the Indian Trust Act, 1882. The trust is required to be separate from the sponsors or the AMC as the unit-holders' funds are to be kept separate from the funds of the AMCs. The proper handling of client's accounts is thus possible.

Sponsor

The sponsor is the company which sets up the mutual fund. Sponsor means anybody corporate who acting alone or in combination with another body corporate establishes a mutual fund after initiating and completing the formalities therefor.

To promote a mutual fund the sponsor has to meet the criteria laid down by the Sebi. These criteria relate to experience, net worth and past tract record in terms of fair dealings and integrity. The sponsor should have a sound track record and experience in the relevant field of financial services for a minimum period of five years, professional competence, financial soundness and general reputation of fairness and integrity in all his business transactions.

Sound track record shall mean net worth, dividend paying capacity and profitability of the sponsor.

Only those who qualify in terms of these criteria are permitted by Sebi to set up mutual funds. The sponsor shall contribute 40 per cent of the net worth of the AMC. The sponsor will not be liable for any loss of the scheme resulting from its operation beyond this initial contribution.

Trustees of the Fund

The management of the mutual fund is subject to the control and superintendence of the Board of Trustees of the Fund. The trustees of the mutual fund are eminent persons who have wide experience in investment matters, finance, administration etc. The Board of Trustees guide the operations of the mutual fund. The trustees carry the crucial responsibility of safeguarding the investors interests. It is their responsibility to see that the AMC always acts in the best interest of the investors.

A company shall be appointed as a trustee to manage the mutual fund. The Sebi may in special circumstances permit the appointment of a board of trustees as trustees of a mutual fund. The appointment of the trustee shall be subject to the following conditions, namely:

(a) the trustees are persons who have experience in financial services and are not found guilty of any economic offence.

(b) the names of the trustees shall be forwarded to the Sebi.

(c) any change in the appointment of the trustees shall be subject to the approval of the Sebi.

(d) no trustee shall retire unless another person is appointed in the place of the retiring trustee.

(e) no person shall be a trustee or a director of a trustee company in more than one mutual fund.

(f) at least fifty per cent of the trustees shall be independent members and no such trustee shall be an affiliate or subsidiary of the sponsor.

(g) an asset management company, any of its directors, officers or employees shall not act as a trustee of any mutual fund.

Instrument of Trust

The instrument of trust shall be in the form of a deed duly registered under the provisions of the Indian Registration Act, 1908 executed by the sponsor in favour of the trustees named in such instrument and shall contain such clauses which are necessary for safeguarding the interest of the unit-holders.

Contents of the Trust Deed

The Trust Deed shall contain the following clauses namely:

1. A trustee in carrying out his responsibilities as a member of the Board of Trustees of the mutual fund shall maintain arm's length relationship with other companies or institutions or financial intermediaries or any body corporate with which he may be associated.
2. A member of the Board of Trustees shall not participate in the meeting of the Board of Trustees or in any decision-making process for any investments in which he may be interested.
3. All members of the Board of Trustees shall furnish to the Sebi the interest which they may have in any other company or institution or financial intermediary or any body corporate by virtue of his position as director, partner or with which he may be associated in any other capacity.

The Trust Deed shall provide for the following:

1. Minimum number of trustees.
2. Trustees shall take into their custody, or under their control all the capital property of the schemes of the mutual fund and hold it in trust for the unit-holders.
3. The unit-holders would have beneficial interest in the trust property to the extent of individual holding in respective schemes only.

4. The trustees shall act in the interest of the unit-holders.
5. It is the duty of the trustee to provide or cause to provide information to unit-holders and Sebi as may be specified by the Sebi.
6. The trustees shall appoint an Asset Management Company approved by the Sebi to float schemes for the mutual fund after approval by the Trustees and the Sebi and manage the funds mobilised under various schemes in accordance with the provisions of the Trust Deed and Regulations. The trustees shall enter into an Investment Management Agreement (IMA) with the Asset Management Company for this purpose. The IMA shall be enclosed with the Trust Deed.
7. Trustee shall take reasonable care to ensure that the funds under the schemes floated by and managed by the AMC are in accordance with the Trust Deed and Regulations.
8. The trustees shall have powers to dismiss the AMC under the specific events only and with the approval of the Sebi in accordance with the regulations.
9. The trustees shall appoint a custodian approved by the Sebi in accordance with the regulations and shall be responsible for the supervision of its activities in relation to the mutual fund and shall enter into an agreement with the custodian for this purpose.
10. The auditor for the mutual fund shall be appointed by the trustees. He shall be different from that of the AMC.
11. It is the responsibility of the Trustee to supervise the collection of any income due to be paid to the scheme and for claiming any repayment of tax and holding any income received in trust for the holders in accordance with the trust deed regulations.
12. The deed shall explicitly forbid the acquisition of any asset out of the trust property which involves the assumption of any liability which is unlimited or shall not result in encumbrance of the trust property in any way.
13. Broad policies regarding allocation of payments to capital or income must be indicated in the Trust Deed.
14. The deed shall forbid the mutual fund, the AMC making or guaranteeing loans or taking up any activity in

contravention of the regulations except with the prior approval of the trustees and Sebi.

Trusteeship fee, if any, payable to the trustees shall be provided. No amendment to the trust deed shall be carried out without the prior approval of the Sebi and unit-holders.

The removal of the trustee in all cases would require the prior approval of the Sebi.

No trust deed shall contain a clause which has the effect of:

(i) limiting or extinguishing the obligations and liabilities of the trust in relation to any mutual fund or the unit-holders, or

(ii) indemnifying of the trustees or the asset management company for loss or damage caused to the unit-holders by their acts of negligence or acts of commissions or omissions.

The Trust Deed shall be available for inspection to any member of public at the registered office or the principal place of business of the mutual fund and if so desired a copy of the same shall be made available to any person on payment of a normal fee as may be decided by the mutual fund.

OBLIGATIONS OF TRUSTEES

Duty to Carry on Business

The trustees shall be responsible for ensuring that the AMC complies with the Sebi (MF) Regulations, 1993. The trustees shall enter into an agreement with the AMC which shall contain the clauses specified in Schedule IV of the Sebi (MF) Regulations, 1993 and such other clauses as are necessary for the purpose of investment of the funds of the mutual fund and such agreement is approved by Sebi. The trustees shall be accountable for and be the custodian of the property of the respective schemes and shall hold the same in trust for the benefit of the unit-holders in accordance with the regulations and the instruments of trust.

The trustees shall take such steps as are necessary to get executed all documents which are necessary to secure the acquisitions, disposals and also ensure that the transactions entered into by the AMC have been properly made and are in accordance with these regulations. Where the trustees have reason to believe that the conduct of business of the mutual fund is not in conformity with these regulations they shall forthwith take such remedial steps as are necessary to rectify the situation and keep the Sebi informed of the same with full particulars.

The trustees shall take steps to ensure that the transactions concerning mutual funds are in accordance with the provisions of the trust deed. The trustees shall be responsible for calculation of any income due to be paid to the mutual fund and also of any income received in the mutual fund for the holders of the units of any scheme in accordance with these regulations and the trust deed.

Power to Obtain Reports

The trustees shall have a right to obtain from the AMC such information as is relevant to the management of the affairs concerning the operation of the trust and may also call for periodical reports from the AMC. The trustees shall receive a quarterly report from the AMC and submit a six monthly report to the Sebi on the activities of the mutual fund.

Power to Call Meetings

The trustees shall call for a meeting of the unit-holders

(a) whenever required to do so by the Sebi in the interest of the unit-holders;
(b) on a requisition of three-fourth of the unit-holders of any scheme or of all the schemes together; or
(c) when the majority of the trustees decide to wind up or prematurely redeem the units or modify any scheme.

Disclosure of Interests

The trustees carry the crucial responsibility of safeguarding the investors interests. Therefore, they should act in such a way that their personal interests do not clash or conflict with the interests of the unit-holders or investors in the administration of the fund. A member of the board of trustees shall not participate in a meeting of the board of trustees or in any decision-making process for any investments in which he may be interested.

Every member of the board of trustees shall furnish to the Sebi the interest which he may have in any other company or institution or financial intermediary or any corporate body by virtue of his position as director, partner or with which he may be associated in any other capacity.

Organisation of Fund

The Mutual Fund will be operated only by separately established Asset Management Companies (AMC). The AMC manages the funds of the various schemes. The AMC plays a key role in running the mutual fund and it operates under the supervision and guidance of the trustees. The AMC is entrusted with the specific task of mobilising funds under the scheme.

Asset Management Company

Asset Management Company means a company formed and registered under the Companies Act, 1956 and approved by the Sebi. The AMC shall be authorised for business by Sebi on the basis of certain criteria and the Memorandum and Articles of Association of the AMC would have to be approved by Sebi. Accordingly, an AMC shall not be registered under the Companies Act without the Memorandum and Articles of Association being approved by Sebi.

Authorised Capital of the AMC

The primary objective of setting up an AMC is to manage the assets of the mutual funds and other activities which it can carry out, such as, financial services consultancy which do not conflict with the fund management activity and are only secondary and incidental. That being so, it may not be practical to expect a company to be set up with a paid up capital of Rs. 5 crores to carry on only incidental activities, without any assurance of its receiving an approval from Sebi to act also as an Asset Management Company for a mutual fund. The Registrar of Company shall not have any objection in registering an AMC if the authorised capital of such a company is approved by Sebi. (Department of Company Affairs Circular No. 4/92 dated 2.9.1992.)

The sponsor or if so authorised by the Trust Deed, the Trustees shall appoint an Asset Management Company which is approved by the Sebi to manage the affairs of the mutual fund and operate the schemes of such fund. The application for the approval of the AMC shall be submitted to the Sebi in

Form A. The Memorandum and Articles of Association of the AMC shall be submitted to the Sebi along with the application for approval. An AMC shall not be registered under the Companies Act without the Memorandum and Articles of Association being approved by the Sebi.

Approval of Sebi

For grant of approval of the AMC, the Sebi may take into account all matters which are relevant to efficient and orderly conduct of the affairs of the AMC and in particular the following:

(a) The existing asset management company has a sound track record, general reputation and fairness in transactions. Sound track record shall mean the net worth, the dividend paying capacity and the profitability of the AMC.

(b) The directors of the AMC are persons of high repute and standing having at least five years of professional experience in the relevant fields, such as portfolio management, investment analysis, financial admini-stration, etc.

(c) The board of directors of the AMC has at least fifty per cent directors who are not affiliated or associated in any manner with the sponsor or any of its subsidiaries or the trustees.

(d) The Chairman of the AMC should not be director of a trustee company or trustee of board of trustees.

(e) The AMC shall have a minimum net worth of Rs. 5 crores. Net worth for this purpose would mean the paid up capital of the company and free reserves.

Affiliate Includes a Company

(i) which directly or indirectly by itself or in combination with other persons exercise a significant control over the Asset Management Company or the Trustee as the case may be.

(ii) in respect of which the Asset Management Company or the Trustee, directly or indirectly, by itself or in combination with other persons exercises a significant control.

(iii) in respect of which significant control is exercised directly or indirectly—

   (a) by persons or

   (b) the relatives of such person or persons whether by themselves or in combination who exercise significant control over the Asset Management Company or the Trustee or

(iv) in which director, officer or employee of the Asset Management Company is a director, officer or employee.

Relative

Relative means a person as defined in section 6 of the Companies Act, 1956 (1 of 1956). In terms of section 6 of the Companies Act, a person shall be deemed to be a relative of another, if and only if—

(a) they are members of a Hindu Undivided Family; or
(b) they are husband and wife; or
(c) the one is related to the other in the manner indicated in Schedule 1A.

SCHEDULE 1A

1. Father
2. Mother (including step mother)
3. Son (including step son)
4. Son's wife
5. Daughter (including step daughter)
6. Father's father
7. Father's mother
8. Mother's mother
9. Mother's father
10. Son's son
11. Son's son's wife
12. Son's daughter
13. Son's daughter's husband
14. Daughter's husband
15. Daughter's son
16. Daughter's son's wife.
17. Daughter's daughter
18. Daughter's daughter's husband
19. Brother (including step brother)
20. Brother's wife
21. Sister (including step sister)
22. Sister's husband

Terms and Conditions of Approval

The grant of approval by the Sebi of the Asset Management Company shall be subject to the following terms and conditions, namely:

(a) the AMC has professional and adequate experience in the management of the mutual funds;
(b) any director of the AMC shall not hold the position of a director in another AMC or of a trustee in any mutual fund;
(c) the AMC shall forthwith inform the Sebi of any material change in the information or particulars previously

furnished which have a bearing on the approval granted by it.

(d) no change in the management of the AMC shall be made without prior approval of the Sebi.

(e) the AMC undertakes to comply with the Sebi regulations.

Termination of Appointment

The appointment of an Asset Management Company can be terminated by majority of the trustees or by seventy five per cent of the unit-holders of the scheme. Any change in the appointment of the Asset Management Company shall be subject to the prior approval of the Sebi.

Restrictions on the Powers

No AMC shall act as a trustee of any mutual fund or AMC of any other mutual fund. The AMC shall not undertake any business activity other than activities like financial services, consultancy, exchange of research on commercial basis as long as any of such activities are not in conflict with the activities of the mutual fund itself without the prior approval of the trustee and Sebi.

A director of the AMC shall not be permitted to hold the position of a trustee in a trust or act as a director in any other AMC.

Not to Undertake Liabilities

The AMC shall not acquire any of the assets out of the scheme property which involves the assumption of the liability which is limited or which may result in encumbrance of the scheme property in any way. The AMC shall not give or guarantee loans or take up any activity in contravention of the regulations.

Operation of the Scheme

The AMC shall take all reasonable steps and exercise all due diligence and ensure that the investment of funds pertaining to any scheme is not contrary to the provisions of the Regulations and the trust deed. The AMC shall be responsible for the acts of commission and omissions by its employees or the persons whose services have been obtained by that company.

No loss or damage or expenses incurred by the AMC or officers of the AMC or any person delegated by the AMC shall be met out of the trust property. Notwithstanding anything contained in any contract or agreement, the AMC or its directors or the officers shall not be absolved of any civil liability to the mutual fund for their acts of commission or omissions while holding such position or office.

Report to Trustees

The AMC shall submit to the trustees quarterly reports on March 31, June 30, September 30 and December 31 on its activities and the compliance with regulations. The trustees shall have the right to obtain from the AMC all information concerning the operations of the various schemes of the mutual fund managed by the AMC at such intervals and in such a manner as required by the trustees to ensure that the AMC is complying with the provisions of the Trust Deed and Regulations.

Disclosure to Unitholders

The AMC shall disclose the basis of calculating the repurchase price and Net Asset Value (NAV) of the various schemes of the fund in the scheme particulars and disclose the same to the investors at such intervals as may be specified by the trustees and the Sebi.

Termination of Assignment

The trustees of the mutual fund may terminate the assignment of the AMC at any time after receiving a reasonable notice in writing from the AMC. The termination shall become effective only after the trustees of the mutual fund have accepted the termination of assignment and communicated their decision in writing to the Asset Management Company. The trustees shall have power to dismiss the AMC under specific events only with the approval of the Sebi in accordance with the regulations.

Custodian

A custodian means a person carrying on the activities of safe keeping of the securities or participating in a clearing system on behalf of the clients to effect deliveries of the securities. The custodian shall not in any way be associated with the Asset Management Company.

The custodian shall be registered with the Sebi. The custodian shall make an application in Form A for registration. For grant of approval of the custodian, the Sebi may take into account all matters which are relevant to efficient and orderly conduct of the affairs of the custodian and in particular the following namely:

(a) the existing custodian has a sound track record, general regulation and fairness in transactions;

(b) the applicant himself or the employees are persons who have experience in providing custodian services.

(c) the applicant has the infrastructure, office space and personnels to provide custodian services.

(d) the applicant or the directors or partner are not found guilty of any economic offence.

(e) the applicant is not the sponsor or trustee of any mutual fund.

The grant of approval to the custodian shall be subject to the following terms and conditions.

(i) the custodian or its director or partners will not in anyway be directly or indirectly affiliated or associated with any AMC;

(ii) the custodian will not act as sponsor or the trustee of any mutual fund;

(iii) the custodian will not act as a custodian of more than one mutual fund without the prior approval of the Sebi.

Shares Held in the Name of Trusts

Section 153 of the Companies Act, 1956 provides that a company's shares could not be held in trust. "No Notice of any trust, express, implied or constructive, shall be entered on the register of members or debenture-holders." This is a mandatory and prohibitory clause. In Bharat Petroleum Corporation Ltd., Stock Holding Corporation of India Ltd., Comp. Petn. No. 175 of 1993 decided on September 23, 1994, the respondent company Stock Holding Corporation of India Ltd., offered custodian services to its clients. The custodian company sougnt to transfer certain shares held in Bharat Petroleum Corporation Limited from its name to Stock Holding Corporation of India (A/c SBI Mutual Fund). The petitioner company refused to register the transfer on the ground that no shares can be held in the name of trust. The Company Law Board held that the shares cannot be registered in the name of Trust. Amendment of relevant provisions of the Companies Act is being contemplated.

Voting Rights

Section 153 A of the Companies Act, 1956 provides that the Central Government may by notification in the Official Gazette appoint a person as public trustee to discharge the functions and to exercise the rights and powers conferred on him by or under the Companies Act.

Where any shares in or debentures of a company are held in trust by any person as the trustee, the trustee shall within such time and in such form as may be prescribed make a declaration to the public trustee.

The provisions of this section shall, however, apply only on the satisfaction of the following conditions:

1. The trust is created by an instrument in writing;
2. The value of shares in or debentures of a company held in trust
   - (i) exceeds one lakh of rupees; or
   - (ii) exceeds one lakh of rupees but does not exceed either five lakhs of rupees or 25 per cent of the paid up share capital of the company whichever is less.

Despite holding large chunks of equity these funds can vote only indirectly through a public trustee appointed by the company. In order to let the mutual funds and the share custodians ensure their best interests, the Central Government has decided to give mutual funds, the right to vote directly in the annual general meetings of the companies in which they hold stake.

8

Securities and Exchange Board of India and Its Performance

The Securities and Exchange Board of India (SEBI) is the national regulatory body for the securities market. It was set up under the Securities and Exchange Board of India Act, 1992 to protect the interests of investors in securities, to promote and to regulate the securities market.

Sebi has its head office in Bombay and it has regional offices in the metropolitan cities of Calcutta, Madras and Delhi. The Sebi board comprises a chairman, two members from the Central government, representing the ministries of finance and law, one member from the Reserve Bank of India and two other members appointed by the Central government.

As per the SEBI Act, 1992, the powers and functions of the board encompass the regulation of stock exchanges and other securities market.

Functions

Sebi performs the following functions:

1. Registration and regulation of the working of stock brokers, sub-brokers, bankers to an issue, trustees of trust deeds, registrars to an issue, merchant bankers, underwriters, portfolio managers, investment advisors and such other intermediaries who may be associated with the stock market.
2. Registration and regulation of mutual funds.
3. Promotion and regulation of self-regulatory organisations.
4. Prohibiting fraudulent and unfair trade practices and insider trading in securities market.
5. Regulation of substantial acquisition of shares and take-over of companies.

6. Calling for information, undertaking inspection, conducting inquiries and audits of stock exchanges, intermediaries and self-regulatory organisations of the securities market.
7. Performing such functions and exercising such powers as contained in the provisions of the Capital Issues (Control) Act, 1947 and the Securities Contracts (Regulation) Act, 1956.
8. Levying various fees and charges.
9. Conducting necessary research for above purposes and performing such other functions as may be prescribed from time to time.

Sebi's Performance

Sebi was set up with the prime objective to protect the investors. It had done little until February 1995. With the appointment of Mr. D.R. Mehta as Chairman, Sebi has gone about incorporating new guidelines to protect investors and also take to task erring market intermediaries, including corporates, who have attempted to mislead investors through incorrect information in public issue documents.

It has taken the following steps to streamline the functioning of stock markets.

1. Sebi has recently drawn up a new set of guidelines to make offer documents more informative for investors. These documents would now give more relevant information, such as, the actual cash-flow status of companies. Also, the shares traded in by promoters over the previous three months would also be mentioned in the documents. However, Sebi has decided on 27th June, 1996 that it will not be vetting offer documents of companies which have a three year track record of dividend payment. Offer documents of companies seeking listing on OTCEI will also not be vetted by Sebi. However, such companies will continue to file their offer documents with Sebi and Sebi will communicate its comments to the issuers and lead managers within 21 days as per present practice for rights issues etc.
2. In another move in the interest of investors, Sebi has stated that projections by companies in offer documents, would be allowed only in cases where the project appraiser has picked up at least 5 per cent stake in the company.

3. Sebi has also directed companies going to raise money through the markets to submit offer document drafts on computer floppies. These floppies would be made available to investors through stock exchanges and Sebi. Such a measure ensures that doubts about the issue are removed before the capital floatation is cleared by Sebi. Adding to this, the regulatory body has instructed all bourses to set up surveillance committees to check price rigging and market manipulation. By doing this, investors are at less risk of being duped by incorrect share prices. Sebi has a cell of its own to look into such market operation violations.

4. Among the most significant moves by Sebi, and the Centre has been allowing the setting up of depositories for which the Depositor's Act 1996 has been passed in the Lok Sabha on 23rd July, 1996 and assented by the President of India on 10th September, 1996. The depositories legislation provides for a central depository, which would be computerised and linked with all stock exchanges.

The depository would keep a check on all share purchases and transfers. More importantly, it will introduce scripless trading. All transfers or purchases of shares would be registered in the central depository. This, holdings would actually be in "electronic scrips" and not in physical scrips, as in practice at present.

It is believed that the central depository would act as a "bank for shares". While guidelines on this system are yet to be finalised, market operators believe that investors would be given pass books, thus officially registering an investor, in which purchases and sales would be recorded. As a result, while the depository keeps a tab on sales of shares, investors would also have a record of their purchases.

The problem of settlements, a near daily problem in most of the bourses would be taken care of by the depository system. Since there would be no physical transfer of securities, settlements could be completed on the day after the purchase. Settlements, according to the Companies, Act are to be completed within 90 days, but in practice, it invariably overshoots this deadline. In addition, other problems such as, bad deliveries would not arise as one would be dealing with electronic scrips.

5. On April 16, 1996, Sebi announced tighter entry norms for the primary market, but retained the threshold limit of a Rs. 5 crores post-issue paid-up capital for companies accessing the capital market. Under the new rules, companies tapping the primary market will have to have a dividend-paying track record for at least three of the five preceding years. However, this new restriction of having a dividend-paying record will not apply to manufacturing companies, whose projects have been appraised by a public financial institution or a scheduled commercial bank, and if such an institution also participates in the project finance and the equity of the issuer.

Sebi chairman D.R. Mehta announced that the board was not in favour of raising the threshold limit to Rs. 10 crores as recommended by the Malegam Committee report. He explained that the raising of the threshold limit to Rs. 5 crores on October 1, 1995, has already had a dampening effect on the number of issues that were flooding the market. He stated that in the first half of 1994-95, the number of new issues were 1,441 while after the amendment of the limit to Rs. 5 crores, there were only 973 issues in the second half.

6. Another significant addition to primary market reforms decided upon by Sebi was a proposed amendment to the listing agreement providing for companies to pay interest to applicants to public issues from the 30th day after the closure of the public or rights issue. At present, companies have to pay interest on the application money if the allotment and refund process is not done within 70 days. Sebi has taken up the matter with the Department of Company Affairs (DCA), after which it will request stock exchanges to amend the listing agreements.

This is aimed as an incentive for the issuer to get the securities listed much faster than at present. Senior executive director, Sebi, C.B. Bhave said the 70-day deadline for listing will continue, but the issuer will have to pay interest on delay in payment beyond 30 days.

7. In a bid to prevent the trend in public shareholding in listed companies steadily going down, Sebi has decided that a norm of five public shareholders for every Rs. 1 lakh of fresh issue of capital and IO shareholders for Rs. 1 lakh of offer for sale may be prescribed as a continuous requirement for being listed. Companies which do not meet this requirement will be given

six months to conform to this. "This will diversify and broad-base the shareholding pattern," Mr. Bhave stated.

8. Sebi has also decided that the minimum subscription limit of 90 per cent will not be applicable to offer for sale and will apply only to outright public and rights issues. This implies that bought out deals done on OTCEI will also be excluded from the minimum subscription requirement.

This move is expected to benefit OTCEI in a big way. About 120 companies have completed bought out deals on OTCEI, but are unable to see the divestment and listing process through. These may get listed easily as there would be no minimum subscription requirement for them.

9. On July 11, 1996, Sebi directed stock exchanges to impose a stringent three-tier margin system aimed at curtailing a build-up of speculative volumes on the bourses. This is the first time that Sebi has recommended comprehensive measures to tackle excess speculation. This was decided at a Sebi meeting with Bombay, Delhi, National Stock Exchange and the Over-the-Counter Exchange of India presidents.

In view of the low percentage of delivery to turnover, Sebi has set a limit on the intra-day trading limits for brokers. According to the Sebi directive, brokers would not be able to exceed 33.33 times the base minimum capital deposited with the exchange. The limits would be applicable on gross basis, that is including purchases and sales.

In case the broker wishes to exceed this limit, additional capital would have to be deposited with the exchange. This capital will not be permitted to be withdrawn for a period of six months. The margin would be payable in cash or bank guarantee on a net basis, without any threshold limit. The margin would be released on the pay-in day for the settlement period. (The guideline is in existence, but has not been enforced rigidly).

Sebi has also decided on a stringent margin system to be implemented by the stock exchanges. These include a mark-to-market margin and an initial margin. Under the mark-to-market margin, the exchange would collect 100 per cent of the national loss incurred by a broker for every scrip on a daily basis. The loss would be calculated as the difference between the buying and selling price and the closing price of the scrip at the end of the day.

Each broker would be subject to a concentration ratio margin payable as an initial margin. The margin would be payable if the gross turnover of a broker for the previous quarter in any three scrips is greater than 70 per cent of his total turnover in all scrips. In such cases, a margin of Rs. 10 lakhs would be payable if the total gross turnover for the first quarter is greater or equal to Rs. 60 crores, but less than Rs. 120 crores. In case the turnover is equal to or exceeds Rs. 120 crores, a margin of Rs. 20 lakhs would be payable.

This margin would be kept with the exchange for one quarter. Exchanges with screen-based trading would have to implement the margins system from the next settlement. Sebi would ask other exchanges, which do not have a screen-based trading system, to implement the initial margin and trading limits after a discussion with them.

10. On July 3, 1996 Sebi announced wide-ranging changes relating to mutual funds. This is likely to affect significantly the way that mutual funds do business and improve the bottomline of mutual funds—most of which are performing none-too-well. The changes will additionally help to pump in liquidity into the market. Mutual funds which had hitherto been allowed to invest only in share markets can dabble in the money market as well.

Most of the proposals announced are contained in the Mutual Funds 2000 report prepared by the Sebi secretariat. These proposals would now be incorporated in the regulations and would become effective from the date of the notification.

Sebi chairman has decided to recommend to the Union government that the Companies Act be amended to enable mutual funds holding shares of companies to have a right to vote in company decisions. This recommendation, if accepted by the government, will vest enormous powers with mutual funds.

All mutual funds would be allowed to launch schemes on the same lines as the Retirement Benefit Plan approved by the government for the Unit Trust of India.

11. The Secondary Market Department of Sebi laid down uniform norms for good/bad deliveries by Press Release on July 16, 1996. The main contents of said Press Release are:

(i) All stock exchanges shall adopt uniform norms for good/bad deliveries which has been laid down by Sebi.

(ii) Each Stock Exchange shall set up a separate Bad Delivery Cell (BDC) latest by 31st September, 1996.

(iii) In the case of deliveries coming under objection, the first introducing broker of the same stock exchange shall be required to rectify the defects/replace the shares along with accrued benefits within 21 calendar days from the date of receipt of the objection and share certificates from the last buying broker of that exchange.

(iv) In the case of inter-exchange bad delivery also 21 days have been allowed for rectification but additional seven days have been provided to forward objections.

(v) In case of dispute Bad Delivery Cell will take final decision.

(vi) What constitutes good/bad delivery has been laid down in Sebi Press Release to avoid any ambiguity and contains 96 conditions. Anyone affected can refer to it.

The standardisation of bad delivery removes a major irritant for the broking community, but even now investors wait for a long for replacement.

12. *The Foreign Institutional Investors (FIIs)*—Ceiling for investment in the listed companies has been raised from 5 per cent to 10 per cent for FII. All FIIs put together can acquire only upto 24 per cent equity in a single company.

In the union budget proposals of July 1996, FIIs have been allowed to invest in the unlisted companies in infrastructure sectors without any ceiling. Opening up of the infrastructure sectors for FIIs was one of the main recommendations of the Rakesh Mohan Committee which recently submitted its report to Union Finance Minister P. Chidambaram.

The aim of this move is that foreign capital flows should not be primarily in the form of portfolio flows only, but also lead to foreign direct investment (FDI) which is more stable and would stay in the country for some years.

However, critics are doubtful that FIIs would be attracted to invest in infrastructure sectors. They do not easily invest in even well run listed private companies with a track record unless there is a sustained bull run. The FIIs in India have been very selective and have invested in about 100 of the 7,500 listed companies.

The FIIs investment record in the infrastructure sectors in other countries has not been satisfactory. Peregrine is under attack for suspected violations in Vietnam. Its cosy deals with Chinese, Burmese and North Korean governments raise eyebrows. Jardine Fleming's brushes with regulatory authorities in UK and Hong Kong are well known. Morgan Stanley's investment strategy in India is nothing short of predatory.

13. *Badla* system led to settlement problems in the stock exchanges. Sebi banned the *badla* system in March 1994. It set up a committee on March 21, 1995 headed by Mr. G.S. Patel, former chairman of the Unit Trust of India to suggest reforms in the stock exchanges and to review the system of carry forward transactions.

Recommendations of Patel Committee

The committee submitted its report on March 26, 1996. It expressed the view that speculative activity is necessary to bring back liquidity in the market and arrest the downward trend in prices. The committee observed that since the ban on *badla,* the daily volumes in specified shares have dwindled to nearly a tenth of the volumes they had registered before the *badla* ban. The committee noted that a large section of transactions had shifted outside the markets and to off-market matched transactions, *i.e.* private deals.

It said: "The stock exchanges are devoid of risk management instruments and also a window for speculative activities, which help in making markets more active, broad and liquid and in improving the climate in primary markets. In fact, the ban on forward trading, in the absence of any better alternative plan in place, for over a year, is proving to be counterproductive in its impact".

The committee stressed the need for speculation as vital for functioning of the market, it has suggested the impounding of 25 per cent profits earned by brokers on their carry-forward business to keep speculation within limits.

The committee pointed out that Sebi itself had permitted forward transactions with prudential norms as spelt out in its letter of March 11, 1994. However, these norms known as the 'twin-track system', were not accepted by brokers.

The Patel Committee says that the Sebi proposal did not take into account the ground realities of our markets and was based on borrowed perceptions. The Committee pointed out that the ingredients of a strong market such as good liquidity, easy availability of bank finance against shares, margin trading, stock lending facilities, depositories, clearing systems and services and electronic data entry systems for execution of investors' orders do not exist in Indian markets.

The committee's main recommendations include the restoration of the carry-forward system with prudential precautions, the continuance of individual carry-forward transactions for 90 days, the resumption of forward trading to be preceded by the facility of screen-based trading to ensure greater transparency, daily segregation of all transactions as those meant for delivery, for jobbing, for carry-forward and trading on own account, impounding of shares received by *vyaj badla* financiers to be kept in safe custody of the exchange to prevent trading in them until the financier is re-paid, separation of brokers' own accounts and those of *vyaj badla* financiers, and permission of payment of contango charges to short-sellers.

The following are the recommendations of the Patel Committee :

(a) Daily margins of 15 per cent on gross position be imposed against the earlier proposal of excessive margins of 30 per cent of the first settlement and climbing to 90 per cent by the fifth settlement.

(b) The margin is to be charged on prices marked to the market on a weekly basis.

(c) Impounding of 25 per cent of the profit earned by the broker on the carry-forward of position.

(d) Squaring up to be permitted between the second and sixth settlement unlike the earlier Sebi stand of carry-forward transactions of delivery or payment as the case may be.

(e) Capital adequacy norms to be enforced effectively.

(f) Resumption of trading in specified shares to be preceded by screen-based trading. BSE given a week to include specified scrips in the BOLT system.

(g) Strong monitoring system be put in place. Stock exchanges to fix responsibility on executive directors for surveillance, audit and reporting.

(h) Uniform settlement period for all stock exchanges.

(i) Sebi could permit the restoration of the carry-forward system with prudential precautions.

(j) The indigenous system of *badla* should not be revised.

(k) Sebi should permit the continuance of individual carry-forward transactions for a period of 90 days (although the committee says, "there does not seem to be any sanctity to limit the performance of a contract in specified shares to 90 days because a contract which is carried forward with the obligations of the previous contract being fully honoured is a fresh contract."

(l) Each transaction carried over from a settlement should be identified by a transaction number which will be continued in every carry-over to ensure that no transaction is carried beyond 90 days.

(m) This safeguard could be implemented by a monthly auditor's report certifying that a broker has not carried forward any transaction beyond 90 days.

(n) The resumption of trading in specified shares should, as far as possible, be preceded by the facility of screen-based trading to ensure greater transparency.

(o) At the end of each trading day, members should be made to demarcate all transactions as those meant for delivery, for jobbing, for carry-forward and trading on own account, and report on these separately. However, trading for transactions meant for delivery need not be conducted separately.

(p) *Vandha* or objection memos of mismatched trades should be rectified the very next day and no *vandha* should be accepted thereafter. The *kapil* (credit note) system should be discarded.

(q) Shares issued by *vyaj badla* financiers should be deposited and kept in safe custody of the stock exchange. This is intended to prevent these shares being traded until the financier has been paid.

(r) Brokers should maintain separate accounts of *vyaj badla* financiers and their own sources of finance.

(s) Payment of contango charges to short-sellers should be permitted as they also perform a useful function in moderating excesses in the markets.

On July 27, 1995, Sebi decided to permit stock exchanges to resume carry-forward trading in shares.

The revised system, though largely based on the recommendations made by the G.S. Patel Committee, is more stringent as it aims at restricting the quantum of forward business. The Sebi suggested system stipulates that carry-forward transactions should not exceed 25 per cent of a broker's total transactions on that day. Also, the rate of daily margins suggested are higher than those proposed by the Patel Committee.

Highlight of New Carry-Forward System

The following were the highlights of the new carry-forward system:

(i) Permission from Sebi to introduce carry-forward.

(ii) Suitable infrastructure, including screen-based trading, and effective monitoring and surveillance system, the responsibility for which to be vested with executive directors.

(iii) Enforcement of a 'twin track' system to segregate carry-forward and cash transactions.

(iv) Identification of each carry-forward transaction by an identity number to be maintained until its final settlement.

(v) Submission of monthly auditor s certificate vouching that there is no violation of the time limits.

(vi) Maximum 90 days for carrying forward of transactions, with facility to square off up to fifth settlement, following which there will be compulsory delivery or payment.

(vii) Daily margins on gross basis: 20 per cent for the first settlement, 30 per cent for second, 40 per cent for third and 50 per cent for fourth and fifth; margins to be marked by the market.

(viii) Carry-forward business should not exceed 25 per cent of a broker's transaction on that day.

(ix) Bar on financiers from squaring up their positions before the share transactions are completed.

(x) Immediate rectification of *vandha* (objection memos) and bar on *kapil* system and *chalu upla* transactions.

(xi) Requirement for brokers to keep records of sources of finance and separate accounts of the finance with sub-accounts with clearing houses.

(xii) Scrip-wise and broker-wise disclosure of carry-forward position at the beginning of carry-forward session.

Some Modifications

The new carry-forward system was rejected by the stock exchanges. On October 5, 1995, Sebi modified new carry-forward system which is as follows:

(a) A flat margin of 15 per cent as recommended by the Patel Committee will be implemented and recovered market-to-market on a weekly basis. This means that if the values of scrips increases, more margins are charged and vice versa;

(b) A capital adequacy norm of three per cent for individual brokers and six per cent for corporates has been stipulated. With the inclusion of this condition, the earlier stipulation on graded margin on carry-forward position and the limit on carry-forward position has been removed. This capital adequacy norm has been accepted by BSE;

(c) Brokers to be allowed self-certification in place of audit as recommended by the Patel Committee. However, Sebi and stock exchanges would be free to run a re-check on the certification;

(d) Mandatory squaring-up of transactions within 90 days; and

(e) Stipulation of publishing the carry-forward position of each broker scrip-wise before the start of each carry-forward session retracted.

Difficulties in Introducing the New System

The modiied system has also not worked. The poor response to the new system can be gauged by the total volume of deals which were carried on July 27, 1996. The dislike for the new system is also reflected in sharp fall in the number of brokers opting for the new system to 149 from over 250 at the Bombay Stock Exchange. The BSE has listed the following difficulties in introducing the new system:

(a) Inconvenience in doing *vyaj-badla* business as clients do not get possession of shares. Besides, shares lying in the clearing house are at the risk of members as there is no insurance for the same.

(b) Unviable *vyaj-badla* operations as members require to pay a charge of Rs. 2 per market lot which works out to 2 to 4 paise per share in most cases.

(c) Difficulties to give effect to special transactions.

(d) Segregation of carry-forward transactions into share *badla*, *vyaj-badla*, etc. because of software related problems in back offices.

Review

Sebi has finally decided to review the carry-forward or *badla* system.

On October 29, 1996 Sebi finalised a series of reforms to boost the suffering stock markets. The measures, including expansion of the Bombay Stock Exchange online trading system (BOLT) and a reduction in the size of minimum applications. The scheme would new allow BSE as well as stock brokers of other exchanges to set up shops in cities where there are no regional stock exchanges.

Terming as an investor-friendly move, Sebi explained that this would immensely improve overall trading efficiency by leading to price formation, price discovery and improved prices for investors especially for thousands of scrips which are only listed on the BSE and nowhere else. This would also improve competition among bourses.

Sebi took care to ensure that smaller exchanges would not be hurt. Though it had been established that the setting up of terminals by another exchange like in the case of NSE, would actually increase total business and not reduce it as it was feared. The apprehension of regional exchanges had to be considered for setting up terminals in such cities. For doing this, the BSE would sign a memorandum of understanding with the regional exchange. In doing this, Sebi explained that the exchange expanding its trading system has to take the following steps:

(a) Ensure that there is adequate monitoring and surveillance mechanism for such outstation terminals.

(b) All such trades would be subject to usual margins, capital adequacy and intra-day trading limits fixed for the brokers by the exchange.

(c) Ensure that investors eventually do not pay the brokerage on such trades exceeding the maximum brokerage permitted as per the rules of the exchange.

(d) Finally, the exchange would introduce the system of guaranteeing trades or set up a clearing corporation.

Accepting that the primary market would be revived and the small investor enticed by reducing the minimum application size from 500 shares or Rs 5000, Sebi reduced the minimum application size from Rs. 5000 to Rs. 2000. Small investors can thus buy, in case of par issues, just 200 shares, while subscribing to a issue.

In a parallel effort to boost the debt market, Sebi has allowed corporates to list debt instruments even if they do not have equity already listed on the bourses. This move is aimed specifically at debt offerings by infrastructure companies. Such companies would typically have large debt components in their financing.

The Sebi board also decided against the fee structure based on "basic management fee" and "additional fees" as prescribed in the NAV committee report following allegation of fund managers that the regulatory body was indulging in micro-management. Instead, Sebi has retained the present two-slab fee structure of the asset management company.

Sebi has allowed mutual fund schemes to borrow to meet payments of dividend and interest (in case of fixed return schemes) too. Earlier, schemes were permitted to borrow upto 20 per cent of the net assets for a period of six months to meet only redemption requirements. The move would help to provide temporary liquidity to the funds.

Sebi also decided to allow the existing asset management companies up to one year from the date of notification of the regulation to increase their networth from the present level of Rs. 5 crores to Rs. 10 crores. It allowed cross trusteeship and cross directorship of independent trustees and independent directors of the board of trustees and board of asset management companies.

It allowed venture capital funds to be set up as companies or trusts and raise money only from institutional investors or high networth individuals.

In the primary market Sebi decided to altogether give up the vetting of offer documents. The vetting of offer documents by Sebi was giving wrong impression in the market that Sebi was approving of the project. Instead, Sebi officials would not focus on inspection to ensure that merchant bankers are exercising due diligence while vetting offer documents.

Sebi has lifted the ban on corporate advertisements, provided risk factors are mentioned. Earlier, Sebi has banned corporate advertisements from the date of issue of acknowledgement card to the date of closure of the issue.

With a view to easing the conditions for putting up large infrastructure projects, Sebi allowed promoters to bring their contributions where it exceeds Rs. 100 crores in a phased manner.

On November 18, 1996, Sebi adopted measures to regulate short selling in the market. It directed the exchanges that a short seller should be asked to declare his position of the short sales at the end of the day. Also, the stock exchange should impose appropriate margin on short sale.

To give effect to the above decision, Sebi decided to set up a group of experts to work out the required modalities. The group would consist of 12 people, including academics and representatives of various stock exchanges.

9

Development of Financial Journalism

Financial journalism grew out of an earlier stage of western economic development which was almost co-terminus with the development of capitalism. At the center of this development was finance. Thus, the capital market, the stock exchange, and corporate affairs like floatations of new companies, declaration of dividends, etc. featured in what is traditionally known as the City Page in the daily newspapers. Later, they became the focus of journals like *The Financial Times* and *The Wall Street Journal.*

Calcutta and Bombay were the centres of the earliest British commercial activity in India and that is where financial reportage also took root. The British managing agency houses engaged in foreign trade and later in industrial ventures and the British merchant banking houses operated mostly from these two presidency towns since the beginning of the 19th century.

Calcutta was important for another reason. It was the Capital of India till 1911. Some of these agency houses also collectively owned newspapers like *The Statesman* and *The Times of India.* Both because of their location and the ownership pattern, were in a position to report the gradual spread of trade and industry in the hinterland.

By the late 19th century, the country had been opened up by railways and telecommunications, Indian enterprise was spreading alongside British enterprise in India, with the consequent spread of interest in financial and commercial information countrywide. It firmly established coverage of these as an expanding activity of the daily press in the interior as well as in the presidency towns. Journals devoted entirely to industry, finance and trade were, however, a 20th century development.

Growth of Financial Magazines for 1888

The Calcutta weekly, *Capital* was probably the first financial journal to be started in India in 1888 by a group of British agency house, some of which were also part owners of *The Statesman*. It was Indianised only when the controlling interest in these firms passed into Indian hands in the fifties and Dinesh Bahl later became its first Indian editor. It reflected mainly the British business viewpoint on the Indian economic affairs and successively British finance members of the viceroy's executive council before independence used it to project their opinion. But *Capital* was not by any means a die-hard paper. Especially under the editorship of Geoffrey Tyson in the forties and fifties, it took a liberal view of such issues as tariff protection, currency, the post-war sterling balances and the emerging Indian public sector.

In its commercial and industrial intelligence it reflected the activities that dominated the eastern region like jute, coal, tea, iron and steel and foreign exchange dealings. Located as it was in the leading British business centre in India, it carried the best informed London financial letter each week. Till the end of the Second World War, London was still the world's financial capital.

The second notable financial weekly, *Commerce* began its publication in 1910 and it was also a Calcutta venture to begin with but was struggling there. It was the British industrialist, Sir Joseph Kay, who gave it a shot in the arm when it moved to Bombay and became a leading financial journal. It owed much in its build-up to R.V. Murthy, its editor in the forties and fifties.

Like its Calcutta contemporary, *Commerce* reflected the business environment of Bombay, made up mainly of its cotton textile industry, foreign trade through its port, and its stock market.

Although Calcutta had a well developed stock market, the Bombay Stock Exchange had come to be accepted since the thirties as the leader in the capital market. Other centres looked to its trading ring in Dalal Street for trends in equities.

With the establishment of the Reserve Bank of India about this time with its headquarters at Bombay that city also became the country's leading financial centre, and *Commerce* had the advantage of direct and instant access to Mint Street.

The first really Indian incursion into the field was *The Indian Finance,* started in Calcutta in 1928, owned and edited by an uncle-nephew team—C.S. Rangaswami and R.R. Srinivas—the two complimented each other admirably.

C.S. Rangaswamy can rightly be called the father of commercial and financial journalism in the country. In the late 1940's his *Indian Finance,* Calcutta, was hardly equalled by the other journals, the *Capital,* Calcutta and the *Commerce* of Bombay. *The Indian Finance* was widely read and respected for its authenticity and wide-ranging articles.

His analysis of Central and State budgets was anxiously awaited and avidly read by everyone. It was said that Central and State finance ministers consulted him while preparing their budgets. It was well-known that Dr. B.C. Roy, the then Chief Minister of Bengal, always consulted him when the State annual budget was prepared. Bengal (undivided) was the first State in the country to ban smoking in Cinema halls. It was generally known that Rangaswamy persuaded the government to enact the legislation.

In his 'Clive Street Gossip' (which was the counterpart of 'Ditcher's Diary' in the *Capital*), C.S. Rangaswamy showed a thorough grasp of the mind of Calcutta's financial district, whose Indian part was mainly Marwari and included such leading houses as Birlas, Jalans, Bangurs, Dalmia, Goenkas and Singhanias. Srinivas had an insight and brought an intellectual flair to his analysis of the changing economic landscape. *The Indian Finance* also carried for many years a weekly dispatch from London by Paul Einzig, a noted British authority of his time on money.

It is not uncommon for the second generation to maintain and build upon the legacy of the founding father. Unfortunately, this was not to be in *The Indian Finance's* case. Its leadership gradually collapsed after Rangaswami's death and Srinivas's retirement for lack of dedication to the task as well as journalistic expertise in a competitive market for financial journalism. The journal died a painful death.

There are a couple of ventures in this line in the years immediately preceding the Second World War or during the war years, like hank's Sundaram's *Commerce and Industry* from Delhi. But they could not survive for want of financial and organisational support. Sundaram, a product of the London School of Economics, was a brilliant man, but if brilliance alone could make a viable financial paper, many papers would have survived.

The next landmark in the economic and financial journalism in India was the establishment of *The Eastern Economist* in Delhi in 1943 and *The Economic Weekly* (now *The Economic and Political Weekly*) of Bombay in 1949. A Birla venture, *The Eastern Economist* was promoted by a business group like the *Capital* and the *Commerce* but was different from both.

Published from Delhi, there was not much of first-hand market intelligence that it could survey. It specialised in analysis and critical evaluation of Indian and International economic affairs and comments on them.

Its first editor, Dr. P.S. Lokanathan, an academician of repute gave the paper an excellent start in this direction. The paper's economic coverage became more extensive as well as specialised under the versatile leadership of Eric de Costa. Its special reports, much on the line of the *London Economist* became a distinctive feature of the paper.

The Paper's character changed rather sharply under V Balasubramaniam's editorship. Its coverage acquired a pronounced political stance more appropriate to a general daily newspaper. It also acquired a magazine format, but neither could save it.

By the early eighties, the daily financial press was well-entrenched and the future was bleak for the weeklies unless they were really different like *The Economic and Political Weekly*. *The Eastern Economist* ceased publication in the late seventies.

The Economic Weekly was launched in 1949. It was virtually a one-man enterprise. Sachin Chaudhuri, who was a lecturer of Economics in the Dhaka University, became the editor of *The Economic Weekly* in 1949. Sachin was an institution in himself. Through his dedication and hard work and without much financial support, he made *The Economic Weekly*, a leading economic magazine in the country. The magazine became so popular that people turned towards it for articles on matters of economic and social interest which were not based in any one particular direction excepting for the national good and in particular the welfare of the weaker sections of the society.

The Economic Weekly became a must reading for all persons who were interested in following the economic progress of the country and the various problems attendant upon the efforts at stepping the growth of the economy.

The Economic Weekly could not survive for long on a tight budget. The advertisements were few and far between. The expenditure would often exceed income. *The Economic Weekly* ceased publication in early 1966.

In August 1966, *The Economic Weekly's* name was changed to *The Economic and Political Weekly*. Sachin could not adapt himself to the new set up and did not show much interest in the new weekly. Sachin died in December 1966.

Sachin led a life of simplicity and austerity. He had put his heart and soul to make *The Economic Weekly* a phenomenal success. The reasonably comfortable existence the journalists are now enjoying would have perturbed him, as would have many other things currently happening in the profession.

Two additions to the periodical press in this category in the seventies were the fortnightlies *The Business India* and *The Business World*, both published from Bombay. The focus of these magazines is on the corporate sector rather than on the economy as such. It was during this period that *India Today*, a popular general fortnightly magazine from Delhi, introduced an excellent section on the state of the economy. This is a prominent case where general magazine journalism made a foray into expert economic writing, much as leading general daily newspapers have done now. *Business Today* has a circulation of 1.6 lakh and *The Business World* 70,000. A new magazine is added to this list by the *India Today* group by bringing in *Business Today* in the 90s. The magazine focuses on management issues and command a circulation of 1.10 lakh copies.

Financial Growth and Their Supplements

The sixties and seventies saw the growth of the daily financial press in India. All the three that came up were from big and powerful newspaper groups.

The Economic Times was the first full-fledged financial daily which was launched by the Bennett Coleman and Company from Bombay in 1961. P.S. Hariharan became the founder editor. Another key person who guided *The Economic Times* in the initial stages was T.K. Seshadri.

In the mid sixties, Dr. D.K. Rangnekar, became its editor. It was he who gave *The Economic Times* a bold editorial style, unafraid of the establishment, showing insight into socio-political developments that were not understood by the well established dailies. *The Financial Express* (Express group) was established in the mid-sixties and *The Business Standard* (Ananda Bazar Patrika group) emerged from Calcutta at the same time.

The spurt in financial journalism has its origin in the liberalisation of the economy.

Liberalisation of Economy

The policy to liberalise the economy was started by former Indian Prime Minister Rajiv Gandhi. Rajiv was keen to usher India into the 21st century.

On November 17, 1984, the Indian government under the leadership of Rajiv Gandhi announced Rs. 10 crores custom duty concessions on electronic goods. Duty on a number of critical inputs like TV glass bulbs and shell and part of rotor assemblies which were already enjoying a concessional rate of duty of 40 per cent *ad valorem* was further reduced to 15 per cent.

Earlier, the Indian government had announced a package of measures in August 1984, including substantial concessions in customs duties in respect of several raw materials, components, sub-assemblies and other equipment to promote the growth of electronics industry. These concessions were further rationalised and liberalised on November 17, 1984. The Indian companies were allowed to tie-up with foreign companies. The consumer market expanded and with it came advertisement boom which helped newspapers to expand their business sections and start new business dailies.

The Indian economy was further liberalised on July 24, 1991 when a new industrial policy was announced.

The highlights of the new policy measures were a substantial reduction in the number of industries requiring compulsory licensing, promotion of foreign investment in India, automatic approval of foreign technology agreements, public sector reform and amendments to the Monopolies and Restrictive Trade Practices Act.

It was decided to do away with the industrial licensing for all industries except 18 specified industries, irrespective of investment levels. The industries where industrial licensing was necessary included areas like coal, petroleum, sugar, cigarettes, motor cars, hazardous chemicals, drugs and pharmaceuticals and some luxury items. Compulsory licensing in these areas were considered necessary for security and strategic considerations, safety reasons and over-riding environmental concerns and the need to regulate production of articles of elitist consumption. Barring these, the entrepreneurs were allowed to freely develop their industries, became more competitive, nationally and internationally.

The theme of the policy was continuity with change. While freedom was given to major industries to grow, reservation of items for the small-scale sector would continue to promote the industrial and agro-industrial employment base.

While proposing major changes in licensing policy, the pre-eminence of the public sector in light core areas would be continued. These included areas like arms and ammunition, atomic energy, mineral oils, rail transport and mining of coal and minerals.

Import of Capital Goods

The new policy envisaged automatic clearance for import of capital goods provided the foreign exchange requirement for such imports was ensured through foreign equity. In addition, with effect from April 1992 when the foreign exchange positions was expected to improve, such automatic approval would be given if the c.i.f. value of capital goods to be imported was less than 25 per cent of the total value of plant and machinery and subject to a maximum limit of Rs. 2 crores.

Existing and new industrial units would be provided with a broad-banding facility to enable them to produce any article so long as no additional investment in plant and machinery was involved. Further exemption from licensing would apply to all existing units for expansion.

The mandatory convertibility clause which enabled financial institutions to convert loans into equity would no longer be applicable for term loans extended by financial institutions for new projects.

Foreign Investment

Direct foreign investment had always been preferred to loans and other forms of assistance. Keeping this in view, the new policy welcomed foreign investment with its attendant advantages of technology transfer, marketing expertise, introduction of modern management techniques in the country and export promotion.

The new policy laid down that from hereafter approval would be given for direct investment up to 51 per cent equity in high priority industries which included 34 broad areas like metallurgy, electrical equipment, transportation, food processing, hotel and tourism industry.

The bottlenecks of any kind for clearance of proposals for foreign equity participation were removed. Such clearance was made available if foreign equity covered the foreign exchange requirement for imported capital goods. In other cases, normal clearance procedures would apply.

Dividends to be expatriated by companies with foreign equity would have to be met through export earnings over a period of time. Foreign equity proposals need not necessarily be accompanied by foreign technology agreements.

Foreign Trading Houses

Companies with foreign equity upto 51 per cent would be encouraged to act as trading houses primarily engaged in export activities. This would generate greater passage of Indian goods to export markets.

Foreign Technology Agreements

In this area, the government proposed to combine the need for updating technology in high priority areas with incentives for domestic sales and export promotion. The policy proposed automatic permission for foreign technology agreements in high priority industries upto a lumpsum payment of Rs. 1 crore, 5 per cent royalty for domestic sales and 8 per cent for exports, subject to total payment of 8 per cent of sales over a 10 years period from the date of agreement or seven years from the commencement of production.

Further, in respect of industries other than those in high priority areas, automatic permission would be given subject to the same guidelines if no free foreign exchange was required for any payments. All other proposals would need specific approval under the general procedure in force.

As regards having foreign technicians or foreign testing in indigenously developed products, no permission is necessary. Payments may be made from blanket permits or free foreign exchange according to the RBI guidelines.

Public Sector

While public sector would continue to play its rightful role in the economy, the government would ensure that it is run on sound commercial lines and continue to innovate and maintain its dominant role in strategic areas.

Towards this end, public sector investments would need to be reviewed. While some reservation of industries for the public sector would be retained, there would be no bar for such areas to be opened up to the private sector selectively. Similarly, the public sector would also be allowed entry in areas not reserved for it.

To raise resources and encourage wider public participation, a part of the government's shareholding in the public sector would be offered to mutual funds, financial institutions, the general public and the workers.

Public enterprises which were chronically sick and which were unlikely to be turned around would, for the formulation of revival or rehabilitation schemes, be referred to the Board for Industrial and Financial Reconstruction (BIFR), or other similar high-level institutions created for the purpose. A social security mechanism would be created to protect the interests of workers likely to be affected by such rehabilitation packages.

The government reiterated its commitment to make the labour force an equal partner in progress and prosperity. The new package provided full protection to the interests of the labour, enhancement of their welfare and upgradation of their skills to equip them to deal with the inevitable technological change. Workers participation in management would be promoted and workers' cooperatives would be encouraged to participate in the efforts to make sick units healthy.

The MRTP Act would be amended to remove the threshold limits of assets in respect of MRTP companies and dominant undertakings.

Emphasis would be placed on controlling and regulating monopolistic, restrictive trade practices. The newly empowered MRTP Commission would be authorised to initiate investigations *suo moto* or on complaints received from individual consumers or classes of consumers in regard to monopolistic, restrictive and unfair trade practices. The amendment of the MRTP Act would eliminate the requirement of prior approval of the Central government for establishment of new undertakings, expansion of undertakings, mergers, amalgamations and take-overs and appointment of directors under certain circumstances.

Multinational Corporations' Entry

The opening up of the economy led to the entry of foreign multi-national corporations (MNCs) and foreign financial institutions into the Indian market. The foreign investors after initial caution and testing the Indian business climate invested in all sectors opened to them. A stable parliamentary form of government, suitable mercantile laws, the English, speaking business culture and above all, a fair and independent judiciary lured them to invest in India.

Consequently, a large number of tie-ups with the foreign companies were witnessed in the major sectors of the economy like the tie-up of Ford, a US automobile giant with Mahindra and Mahindra. General Motors (US) is collaborating with the Hindustan Motors (Birlas) for its Opel Astra, Telco (Tatas) with Mercedes Benz (Germany), the French Giant Peugeot with Premier Automobiles, Daewoo (S. Korea) with DCM (Bharat Ram) for Cielo, Hyundai, another Korean auto giant has decided to invest $ 1 billion in India, Sipani Motors with Rover Montengo.

Hinduja group, together with Ashok Leyland have reached an agreement with Toyota Corporation and Daihatsu Motor Ltd. of Japan to study the feasibility of manufacturing passenger cars in India.

One of the new cars which is likely to command a substantial size of the Indian market and pose a danger to Maruti 800 is a small car to be manufactured by Eicher group in collaboration with the French car-maker, Chatenet. The Fiat UNO—a four-door 1000 cc car was launched by PAL in collaboration with Fiat (Italy). The Fiat group has a plan to launch its world car in India soon. The company expects the world car to sell more than 1 million per year. The car would be manufactured in South America, Poland, Morocco, South Africa, China and India.

In the telecom sector, giants like AT & T (US), Motorola (Japan) and Nokia (Finland) have made an appearance on the Indian scene.

IBM, the US Computer giant, has tied up with Tatas. In the electronics sector Sony, Samsung, National, Japanese companies have made massive forays into the Indian markets.

In the consumer sector, Kelloggs, Pepsi, Coke, McDonald, Kentucky, Baskin Robins, Revlon, Adidas, Nike, Reebok, Lacos and Bennetton have made an entry.

Top foreign designer, such as Pieree Cardin (French), Gian Franco Ferre and Versache (Italian) have also entered into collaborations.

The post-liberalisation period not only increased the circulation of business dailies, but also improved their quality. There was a massive increase in the circulation of the main financial dailies.

The All-India production figures of the main financial papers are as follows:

The Economic Times	3.5 lakhs
Business Standard	60,000
The Financial Express	45,000
Business and Political Observer	18,000
Business Line	26,000

The circulation figures were less than half of the present numbers in the 1980's. The launching of *Business Today* by the *India Today* group, the emergence of the *Business and Political Observer* (Reliance group), *Business Standard* (Delhi) and the *Business Line* in the 90's confirmed the increasing demand for business news. Success of magazines like the *Dalal Street Journal* and the appearance of small newspapers like *Money* and *Financial Wizards* confirmed this trend.

The general newspapers increased the coverage of business news from half page to four pages. *The Telegraph* and *The Asian Age* have separate business pullouts. *The Times of India* and *The Hindustan Times* have enlarged sections covering business news. *The Statesman* is the last one to join this group and also increased the coverage from half a page to four pages.

On the quality front, the first change in this direction was the changing of the colour of the financial dailies from white to pink. The idea was to give it a different individuality and style as also to identify the business dailies from the political dailies. They modelled it on the *Financial Times* London pattern. *The Economic Times* changed its colour to pink in 1990, *Financial Express* in September 1994 and *The Business Standard* in mid-1994.

To give more momentum to reporting on stock and corporate areas, professionals like chartered accountants and MBAs were employed to visit the companies' plants and analyse their performance.

Additional supplements are being carried by *The Economic Times, The Business Standard, The Financial Express* and others to focus on markets and advertising, stock markets, corporate styles and money and finance.

For example, the aforesaid dailies carry the following supplements:

The Business Standard	Smart Investor (Mondays)
	The Strategist (Tuesdays)
	Money Manager (Thursdays)
	Corporate (Saturdays)
The Economic Times	Investor's Guide (Mondays)
	Brand Equity (Wednesdays)
	Corporate Dossier (Fridays)
The Financial Express	Investor (Saturdays)
	Brandwagon (Fridays)

The credit for revamping *The Economic Times* in 1990-92 goes to T.N. Ninan, a Syrian Christian from Kerala and a product of Presidency College, Madras. Ninan made an impact as the Business editor of *India Today* in the 80's. As a result of his efforts, for the first time, a business section in a magazine received an identity of its own.

The business section of the *India Today* was professionally packaged and snappily written. Macro-trends in the Indian Economy were noted along with takeovers and emerging executive lifestyles.

As a formula, it clicked. Ninan, in a way, epitomises the supernova of business publications.

The Economic Times emerged from an eight-page to a 24-page newspaper. It is true that part of the reason for new feature sections and the redesigning of the product was due to the threat from the then to be launched *The Business and Political Observer*. But there is no denying the fact that Ninan with his loyal and devoted team gave the paper a dynamic leadership and a sense of urgency to help it retain its position as a market leader.

Ninan is a professional and a disciplinarian. He is impetuous, hard working and has a penchant for details. To rise from the level of a sub-editor from the commerce desk in *The Hindustan Times* in mid-seventies to the position of the Executive Editor of the largest circulated financial daily speaks volumes for his initiative and drive. He deservedly got the B.D. Goenka award for excellence in business journalism.

The credit for revamping *The Financial Express* goes to Prabhu Chawla who virtually put the paper on its feet from a shamble.

There were three major factors which led to business journalism boom. They are as follows:

1. People wanted to save money to beat inflation. A new class of middle level executives and professionals emerged with higher pay packets who could spare money for investment. Equity cult started by Reliance in 1980's picked up fast.
2. People were keen to make quick buck and were not interested in making investment in traditional areas.
3. Boom in consumer sector, a lot more to buy.
4. Advertisement boom, a Rs. 5000 crore market in the post-liberalisation era.

Today, there are 26 stock exchanges in India, 24 of these are officially recognised, two stock exchanges, that is Sikkim and Gwalior are not recognised. In addition to these 24, two more exchanges were set up. The Over the Counter Exchange of India (OTCEI) and the National Stock Exchange.

There are 8000 companies registered on the stock exchanges, whereas they were merely 3000 in 1980. The capitalisation in the stock market amounts to rupees four lakh and fifty thousand crores from merely Rs. 90,000 crores in 1980.

The number of investors has gone up from 20 million to 50 million. The Foreign Institutional Investors (FIIs) have invested nearly Rs. 14,000 crores in the stock markets and this investment is likely to go with the sweeping changes that are being brought about in the stock markets. There are more than 100 FIIs who have made their presence in India.

Invasion of Foreign Media Networks

The interest taken by foreign media networks in the Indian business climate further confirms the boom in the business journalism in India. Foreign media networks have sent hordes of correspondents to the Indian sub-continent to report and give wide coverage to the corporate sector changes, mega mergers, joint ventures that is changing the business face of India. The Confederation of Indian Industry (CII) Centenary Celebrations in Mumbai in January 1995 saw a plethora of North American press and other media corps.

The happy augury is that almost all the important media networks have set up full-fledged bureaus in India to cover the cataclysmic changes in the Indian sub-continent. *Bloomberg Business News, AF Asian Financial News, Knight Ridder Financial India, Don Jones Telerate, The Asian Wall Street Journal, The Far Eastern Economic Review* are now operating in full strength.

Reuters has been in India for over a century now. It is the leading international news and business information organisation. Reuters has a full-fledged bureau in Mumbai and Delhi with a team of around 20 correspondents and stringers at both the places. Reuters is constantly adding to the network and will soon set up permanent staff bureaus in Calcutta, Madras and Bangalore. But its strength is derived from around 30 stringers posted all over the country, especially in places where it is not possible to have a proper functioning bureau.

Since most of the news being disseminated, is centered around the stocks, debts and the growing commodities market. Reuters recruits business and financial journalists with at least two years reporting experience. There are also openings for dedicated equity researchers as well as economists. This is a pointer for journalists and researchers working in the research bureaus of *The Economic Times, Business Line, Business Standard, Financial Express* and the capital market. Reuters will now concentrate on shipping, transport and infrastructure news and are on the look out for specialists.

But according to a senior Reuters source, Reuters Financial Television will be the key component of Reuters activities in India. For example, press conferences in the Reserve Bank of India's auditorium will be covered live and global dissemination of important policy changes will be faster than the printed word. Honk Kong is the Asian headquarters for the Reuters. This is the base for training, and every year at least three to four Indian journalists are sent there for a month's intensive programme.

The heavy weight, Dow Jones and Co. after setting up a liaison office in India in 1994 is steadily increasing its operations. The U.S. based Dow Jones is a leading publisher of business daily news. The global business daily, *The Wall Street Journal Europe* and the *Asian Wall Street*, have a worldwide circulation, which exceeds 2 million. *Dow Jones'* other publications include Barron's *Far Eastern Economic Review, The Wall Street Journal* Classroom Edition, *Smart Money* (a highly successful personal financial magazine) and *American Demographics*. But Indian journalists will be interested more in *Dow Jones Telerate* which is fast expanding its activities in India.

Dow Jones Telerate is a supplier of real-time market data and news to the international financial community. It has recently launched a customized version of Telerate's information and serves on a single terminal. It provides the full range of *Dow Jones Telerate's* real time historical market data. Mike Mallory is the chief correspondent of *Dow Jones Telerate* and he has been entrusted to set up a full functioning bureau in India.

Says Mallory, "Currently we have two reporters specialising in the money market. We are looking for more equity corporate reporters. Experience in financial reporting is a must. We plan to increase the size of our Delhi operation. Calcutta, Madras and Bangalore is next on the agenda. As for salaries, we tend to look at the prevailing local wages and pay a little more. But again our salaries are more competitive world-wide".

AFX-Asia Financial News is increasing its presence in India, though it is still playing the wait and watch policy. The shareholders in AFX-Asia PTE. Ltd. are Agence France-Press

(AFP), the oldest international news agency in the world, the *Financial Times* group which publishes the revered *Financial Times,* Australian Association Press, a consortium of 14 newspapers, AFP-Extel News Ltd. and Nikei which publishes Nihon Keizai Simbun, the worlds largest circulated economic newspaper with some three million readers. Tony Tassell is stationed as the Mumbai correspondent. There might be two more stationed in Delhi soon.

Richard Baum of Bloomberg Business News is excited about the Indian capital market and foresees a strong *Bloomberg* presence in India soon. *Bloomberg* provides news about the financial and commodities market. Knight-Ridder Inc., a leading information and communication company set up in India two years ago now has a string presence in India. According to Alok Jha, business development manager, *Knight-Ridder-Financial India,* has more than 20 reporters in India Knight-Ridder prefers people with over five years experience in business and financial journalism. *Knight-Ridder Financial,* a part of the Kansas based Knight Ridder Incorporation operates 24 hours a day from 30 bureaux worldwide, providing a range of specialist real time information services, exclusive news and analysis to the world financial market.

Opportunities for the Indian journalists are not confined to the Indian shores only, the Gulf region is suddenly seeing a fresh boom in business and political newspapers and the demand for the Indian journalist is tremendous. *The Khaleej Times* and *The Gulf News* is flooded with Indian reporters. The new publications like *Doha News* and *Gulf Today* are expected to see further exodus of the Indian journalists to the Gulf.

Meanwhile in the East, Asia Inc. Ltd. and Manager Group of Bangkok which owns the two premium brands Asia Inc. and Asian Advertising and Marketing is flexing its muscles. *The Asia Times* is the new publication. Asia Inc. has been doing sorties on India. This organisation is on the look out for stringers and correspondents.

Interestingly, the prestigious American Management Association has belatedly earmarked India as the future hotbed of management practices and soon plans to see a Management Development Forum here. Many specialist management publication are slated to be published from India. The consequent demand for management writers, especially from Corporate Dossier, *The Strategist, Business World, Business Today, Business India, Business Line* is on the cards.

Another feature that distinguishes the foreign business media networks from the India media network are the advanced gadgets and facilities provided to journalists. Most senior correspondents are provided with laptops. Mobile phones are given to all roving correspondents. Facsimiles/modems are also provided to journalists operating from their homes.

With heavy weight publications like *Euromoney Global Finance,* the *Institutional Investor, Financial World, Asia Money,* the *Advertising Age* are expected to station full time correspondents in India. This would add to the burgeoning demand for Indian journalists.

The Boom in Advertising Sector

Many economists and social scientists have drawn parallel of the boom in business journalism with the boom in the advertising industry. The boom in the Indian advertising which began in the early nineties, has kept pace with the fizz by recording a phenomenal growth of 49.5 per cent in 1994-95, higher and above the growth rates of 36.5 per cent and 37.4 per cent recorded in the previous two years respectively.

The Hindustan Thompson Association (HTA) has retained its position at the top, recording a 40.2 per cent growth in 1994-95. Its capitalised billing stands at Rs. 410.69 crores with Lintas following behind with a 38.9 per cent rise at Rs. 339.44 crores. The report by the A&M magazine, reveals that the third position is held by Mudra with Rs. 240.19 crores, the fourth and fifth position are held by Ogilvy and Mather which was propelled by a growth rate of 54.8 per cent to touch Rs. 188.51 crores and Ulka which touched Rs. 154.07 crores, a growth of 40 per cent.

The report states that three agencies in the top ten grew by more than 70 per cent—Trikaya Grey (78.2 per cent for Rs. 117.02 crore), Contract (79.2 per cent for Rs. 113.38 crore) and MAA Bozell (80.8 per cent for Rs. 108.91 crores). In the top 25, Concept more than doubled its business (111.9 per cent) to Rs. 85.82 crores. IB & W, which was 45 in 1992-93, grew by 141.2 per cent in 1993-94 to move up to 35 and with a growth of Rs. 221.3 per cent in 1994-95 stands at 22 with capitalised billing of Rs. 40.16 crores.

The A&M magazine analysis has revealed that the biggest contribution to the spurt in 1994-95 has been Mumbai with the billing growing by 72.3 per cent whereas in the earlier years, billing has grown faster in Delhi compared to Mumbai, which the report describes as "a slowpoke between 1990-92", saw a good year in 1993 but the following year again a slowdown.

Similarly, Bangalore which did not do much in 1990-92, saw the growth figure leap upto 68.8 per cent in 1992-93 before subsidising subsequently, but then picked up again in 1994-95. The report finds that growth in Madras has been steadier than in Bangalore, barring 1991-92 when it slumped to 16.4 per cent. However, it says that Madras grew faster than Bangalore in three years out of five. Calcutta's record has been described as "tame in comparison". Hyderabad, the newest metro to emerge as a major centre, has recorded strong growth on a small base, however, in every year barring 1992-93 Its best year, in percentage terms, was 1991-92 when it was 70 per cent.

A remarkable feature is that while national growth has followed a clear pattern of increased acceleration each year, the same is not true for any of the metros except Delhi. R.K. Swamy/BBDO, which has dropped two ranks to eight, while Rediffusion DY&R (24.8 per cent) and Chaitra Leo Burnett (29.9), have recorded relatively lower growth rates to slip by three and two ranks respectively.

Boom in Business Electronic Media

Before 1990 there was hardly any programme devoted to the business and finance on television network in the Indian sub-continent. A few discussion in the certain programmes on economic policies and business was main part of the limited coverage given to it. The onset of the liberalisation and economic development saw a virtual boom in the business electronic media. Business software (business programmes) was given special stress, and it began to occupy the prime time to the national network and the satellite channels.

Programmes like Crossfire, Rajinder Few Rupees More, India Business World on DD and India Business Report on

Star TV enjoyed high viewership. This prompted other satellite channels to cash in on this market leading to a flood in business software. Its popularity can be gauged by the launching of the channels exclusively devoted to the business and finance in India and abroad like the Money channel and ABNI.

These channels are able to score over the business newspapers as they have the constant interactive, on-line news with visual elements. This means as a day progresses viewers get an updated in-depth analysis of business transaction and events along with interviews.

Boom in Vernacular Business Journalism

The boom in vernacular business journalism has given an overall impetus to the business journalism as a whole. Media Mughal Rupart Murdoch has said that the future of journalism in India lies in its diversification into the vernacular journalism. The Gujarati version of *The Financial Express* has the highest circulation than at any other centre. The Gujarati financial daily *Vapaar* has a tremendous following in the Western India, so is the Hindi business paper *Bhav Thav* published from Indore. The launching of the first national business daily in Hindi by the Amar Ujala group *Karobar* only confirms the statement made by Mr. Murdoch. Even Mark Tully, the ex-bureau chief of the B.B.C., who during his tenure in India, travelled the length and breadth of this country concluded that for the complete growth of journalism in India the vernacular journalism will have to be developed at a rapid pace.

The *Amar Ujala Karobar,* which was launched in 1995 became the first national business daily in Hindi. The paper shows the growing interest of the people in non-English business daily. The paper has 16 pages and is available on all days except Sundays. On Wednesdays, it has special four-page coloured supplement for the readers to get a comprehensive reading from their paper. The supplement is called *Kalpavriksha* and contains stories other than those which are business-related. *Karobar* started initially as a four-page pullout of the Hindi political daily *Amar Ujala* which gave mainly corporate news, commodity rates and kept major stress on the share markets with share quotation and the analysis of various companies. The eagerness shown by the readers of this paper for greater business coverage prompted the *Amar Ujala* group to publish the *Amar Ujala Karobar* from six centres in India.

The editor of the *Amar Ujala Karobar,* Mr. Mandirata, claims that his paper will give the reader more knowledge about the financial and business news than the English daily. According to Mr. Mandirata, their newspaper will give the reader in-depth analysis of the stock market, behind the scene business activity and complete news on corporate affairs.

10

Economic Reporting

What is Economic Reporting

The reporting of a business or financial event or chain of events constitutes business reporting. It is distinct from non-business news items like political or social events. Today, even sports will qualify as business or financial journalism as sports events are being sponsored by big companies to promote their products.

News reporting in business journalism can be split into reporting on policy stories or on corporate stories. A policy story will consist of changes in the rule and regulations or general issues which have an effect on the economy and the companies in various industries. For example, a change in the Exim policy and its effect on the public as well as the industry, or the government decision to withdraw 40 per cent foreign stake in the domestic airlines will be policy stories.

Corporate stories have reports mainly about companies performance, expansion and merger with other companies or foreign tie-ups or split of family groups. To present the complete corporate business climate, a good example is the recent news about the Indian corporate giant ITC which has been asked to pay a mega excise penalty of Rs. 800 crores. This will have effect on their profits and consequently on their share price, involving investors and ultimately snowballing into an issue which will interest the reader.

Difference Between Economic and General Reporting

Difference in the treatment of the story depends on the reader of the political and financial newspaper. If the reader buys a financial paper in addition to a political daily, he spends twice and apparently possess sound economic background. He may be a small but serious investor. More than the general news, he may be interested in columns on investment opportunity or how to save money from tax or ideas to beat inflation. If the reader gets business news from general papers he is not only interested in political news but also wants information on his odd lot of shares, new investment units, life insurance or anything that has an economic tag attached to it. He is a typical salaried employee usually in the government sector.

Economic journalism has become in the last decade extremely demanding in its expectations from its practitioners. Politics may still be the staple diet of most newspapers in India, but it can safely be said that the range of concerns and the technical complexities of the issues that an economic journalist has to master are infinitely more exacting than what a political reporter has to.

An economic reporter has to know a great deal more about his subject, than a general reporter. An economic reporter needs keener eye for the awkward fact that lies buried under a lot of gobbledegook and a sharper nose to smell out hanky-panky.

An economic reporter needs a good grounding, not so much in the academic economics, as in the mechanics of an economy in operation. For this, a structured course is suggested either self-organised or organised by many institutions that profess to train journalists.

The basic reading should include a good textbook of economics and the other on the Indian economy, half-a-dozen other source-books that explain how the various economics, fiscal and other monetary institutions and mechanisms function and how official policies are made. I would suggest that people in the economic ministries and in the corporate sector should be asked by these journalists training institutions to give lectures on both the theoretical and practical aspects of their work as a part of the structured course.

Every newspaper that recruits reporters and sub-editors should send them at their cost to these institutions to attend courses. There should also be refresher courses for updating the knowledge of senior staff. A similarly structured course on an industry, with a discussion on the issues in each individual industry, should be a part of the professional education of an economic journalist.

The days that one learnt on the job and was a versatile amateur, doing the crime beat one day, and commerce and industry the next, are definitely over. Not that economics is atomic physics, obstruse and mind-boggling, but the details that one has to master, the technological and the techno-economic dimensions that one has to grasp, are complex. And given the fact that economic reporter's job is often to bring into open what government and other would much rather hide, it is necessary that he has a firm mastery of the areas of his concerns.

Accuracy should be considered as the most important characteristic of a reporter, particularly an economic reporter. This means that a reporter should inform himself about the subject as thoroughly as he can. This is not easy. Economics is becoming more and more differentiated and specialised. Developments in the economy are also becoming more and more complex and received wisdom and venerated dogmas have failed both as explanations and solutions.

A newspaper man is not an expert and should not pretend to be one. But he should acquire enough grounding to enable him to follow the developments in the economy and have a logical enough mind to spot evasions and attempts to mislead. A certain amount of specialisation will help but the important thing is that he should have a basic understanding of the structure of the economy he is reporting on. This means acquaintance with broad statistics and issues relating to it.

A journalist, especially a reporter, lives by picking other people's brains, both in order to get news leads and to check the accuracy of what is being told to him. He should be for over a guard against "plants", of being made use of rather than his making use of the source.

Example of a Plant

CZECH Ties with India set to Expand'—New Delhi, October 27, 1993; The Czech Republic is a small, young country. It came into existence on January 1, 1993, when the Czech and the Slovak people decided to have a velvet divorce and separate with mutual consent as friends. Exactly 75 years earlier, they had created Czechoslovakia. In 1919, Ruthenia joined in it. With the establishment of two sovereign states—the Czech Republic and the Slovak Republic—an era spanning three quarters of a century came to an end.

The Czechs and the Slovaks are two branches of the same family. They speak similar languages. They have both suffered under foreign domination. It is gratifying to note that they separated without any ill feeling. Looking at the suicidal civil war in Yugoslavia, this is no mean achievement.

On January 1 this year, when Czechoslovakia faded into history and was replaced by two independent states, there were no official celebrations in the Czech Republic. The Czech Prime Minister, a champion of the free market, rebuffed proposals by his Slovak counterpart, a former communist, for a non-specified political confederation and for a slower pace of economic reform. The Slovak Prime Minister had promised voters a slower and less painful disengagement from central planning.

The Czech Republic is merely the rebirth of a country known as the "lands of the Czech crown". The legacy of the old Czech kingdom and the 1,000-year heritage of the Czech state have left an indelible imprint on the culture and history of many European nations.

Commercial relations between our two countries have a long history, the beginning of which dates back to World War II. These relations became more extensive in the late 1950s when India went in for industrialisation in a big way.

In the background of major Indo-Czech projects, Skoda played a significant role. Skoda India was established in India in 1930 and its substantial involvement in Indo-Czech trade continues till now.

On a personal note, I am delighted to be able to represent my country in India. I am no stranger to India. I have visited this country 20 times since 1959. I call these visits pilgrimages. The subject of my doctoral research in the university was Indian rural novels.

I enjoy composing poems in Hindi, nine volumes of which have been published. I also know Marathi, Gujarati and Bengali.

This story should have been outrightly rejected by the Chief Sub-Editor. The author of this write-up is just trying to gain publicity for himself and his country. This item is fit to go as an ad or as a part of a sponsored feature by the Czech Embassy in India.

Another Example of a Plant

New Delhi, March 20 1997: Delhi Chief Minister Sahib Singh Verma did not exactly endear himself to the Nepalese during his recent visit to the country.

At the inauguration of the India Trade Exhibition on March 14 in Kathmandu, where the King and the Queen of Nepal as well as its Prime Minister and senior officials were present, Mr. Verma created a stir by saying, "I am very fond of Nepalese. My servant is a Nepalese and he is like a family member." Not surprisingly, this didn't go down well with the Nepalese.

The fair was organised jointly by the Indian Trade Promotion Organisation (ITPO) and the Confederation of Indian Industry (CII), to show case India's products in Nepal and to promote bilateral trade and economic relations between the two countries. However, the remark by Mr. Verma, according to those present took the cordiality out of the occasion.

"The reaction to this statement was terrible," said an Indian industrialist who was present at the inauguration. "When I heard the Chief Minister say this, I wished I was not there."

According to sources, Mr. Verma's remarks were highlighted by the vernacular press in Nepal.

Reacting to the gaffe, several Indian industrialists, who had gone specially to Kathmandu to attend the fair, said such unthinking statements made by politicians defeated the efforts made to forge cordial ties with neighbouring countries.

"As it is, there is a feeling in Nepal that India tries to play the big brother. Such remarks only intensify these feelings and show that we are insensitive. The Chief Minister did not mean any malice, but he should have been careful," said an Indian CEO.

An official delegation led by Commerce Minister Mr. B.B. Ramaiah, and a high-powered business delegation led by CII president, Mr. Shekhar Datta, had gone to Kathmandu to attend the exhibition. Other members of the business delegation included Mr. Subodh Bhargava, Mr. R.C. Bhargava, Mr. Dhruv Sawhney, Mr. K.N. Shenoy, Mr. Jamshed Godrej, Mr. Rajive Kaul and Mr. Tarun Das.

The official delegation included the chairman of the ITPO, Mr. K.K. Mathur, as well as senior officials of the Commerce Ministry. Representatives of several Indian companies taking part in the exhibition were also present.

Some members of the delegation are of the view that the government should give special training to politicians and teach them how to conduct themselves when they go abroad.

The reporter in the above case had Congress leanings and he wanted to show Delhi's Chief Minister Sahib Singh in poor light. Even if Sahib Singh had committed such a grave mistake, there was no need to blow it beyond proportions and highlight it. Since our national honour was involved, the reporter should have realised his social responsibility and played down the news. A reporter should not play into the hands of vested interests.

On September 23, 1996, a leading financial daily carried a lead story on the corporate performance in India. The reporter did not check his facts and wrote that the Bharat Heavy Electricals Ltd. has shown negative growth rate. In fact, BHEL is among a few public sector undertakings which has performed extremely well and is capable of competing with the best electrical equipment manufacturing companies in the world. It had also declared 20 per cent dividend.

The publication of this report was totally devoid of accuracy and led to a lot of criticism. The top brass of the BHEL descended on the paper, met the editor and asked for an immediate publication of a correction in the newspaper.

On September 24, 1997, the following letter by the General Manager of BHEL was carried. It read as follows:

"Factually Incorrect

This is to draw your kind attention to certain factual inaccuracies in the news item titled "Corporate India to report sharp drop in sales growth" (ET, September 23). In the report, classification of BHEL as "laggard" with 16 per cent decline in performance is based on factually incorrect data and is not fair to BHEL.

As a matter of fact, the turnover of Rs. 1,483 crores as reported was registered by the company in the five months ended August 1996 and not six months ending September 1996, as mentioned in your news item. The performance of BHEL during the corresponding period of five months of the last year was Rs. 1,361 crores which clearly established the upward growth rate of performance.

The actual figures of turnover upto September 1996 will be known only at the end of this month, but the present trend indicates that it will definitely be more than Rs. 1,776 crores achieved last year, which further establishes the upward growth trend of BHEL performance.

In the same news item, it has been reported that "BHEL will suffer on account of lower orders". The factual position is that despite growth in turnover, BHEL's order book as on date, exceeds Rs. 10,000 crores—the highest so far. In the first half of the current financial year, the company has so far secured new orders worth Rs. 4,200 crores, which is highest for any year. In the light of this, the contention in your news item that BHEL will suffer because of lower orders is not borne out by facts".

Anirudh Singh, General Manager (CC), BHEL, New Delhi, September 24.

A reporter of a financial daily went to interview Mr. L.M. Thapar, a leading industrialist. After the interview was practically over, the reporter asked Thapar whether he was going to relinquish the chairmanship of his group to Vikram Thapar, his nephew. Thapar gave an elusive reply and said that he did not know and that he had not decided.

The newspaper carried the story on January 30, 1996 with the headline that "L.M. Thapar to step down from KCT". It was promptly denied by Thapar and by other newspapers.

These days the young reporters are more keen to do exclusive stories and quickly get bylines. They want to be on a fast track to catapult themselves into prominence. They need experience and guidance to undertake this kind of work. They lack both. That is why there are many denials of such stories. Such denials erode the credibility of the newspapers and should be avoided. It is absolutely essential that the senior correspondents should check the copy of the young reporters and guide them.

News Sense

Next to accuracy, an economic reporter must have discernment to spot news in the flood of material that threatens to drown him. There are literally hundreds of studies and analytical papers which are rich in news leads and which are otherwise useful. But it requires skill and patience to learn to use them.

Objectivity

This is important not in the sense of involvement but in the sense of holding balance even between two rival interests. A respect for facts will save one from many an error and prejudice.

The first task for an economic reporter is to focus on the economic aspect of the news. When the major political parties hold their annual conferences, they pass a host of resolutions, but the most important resolutions for the economic reporter is a resolution on economic issues. Even in their routine meetings, the political parties discuss their stance on burning economic subjects, the economic reporter should focus his stories on these projections.

Examples

Left Warns Against Full Deregulation – New Delhi, February 28, 1996: Another front has been opened in the war between the liberalisers in the United Front and the Left with the latter strongly opposing the government's move to completely dereserve the small-scale sector in the light of the Abid Hussain Committee recommendations.

Both the CPI(M) and the CPI have reacted with alarm saying that Industry Minister Murasoli Maran would be well advised not to rush with the 'disastrous' recommendations of the Committee such as dereserving the entire small-scale sector and removing the 24 per cent foreign direct investment ceiling.

The CPI central secretariat member, Mr. Atul Kumar Anjaan asked: "Why is the industry ministry in such a hurry to invite foreign investment in all sectors, particularly in the small sector"?

The CPI(M), too, flayed Mr. Maran's 'enthusiasm' to "destroy one of the India's foundations of economic independence". Senior Marxist MP Hannah Mollah said: "Any attempt to deregulate the small-scale industry and open it up to foreign investors would be at the cost of those dependent on it for their livelihood".

PDS Issue Price Increase to Compromise Scheme for Poor

New Delhi, February 19, 1996: The pulls and pressures within the United Front on the food subsidy issue have taken on a bizarre aspect. A compromise formula being worked out seeks to raise the issue price of foodgrains before providing it at half that price to people below the poverty line. For the intended beneficiaries of the scheme, it amounts to being given with one hand and deprived with another.

The move is designed to keep both the finance minister and the Left happy by adopting a middle path. By raising the issue price before supplying it at half that price, the overall subsidy burden is sought to be contained.

Under the latest proposal, the central issue price for wheat has sought to be increased to Rs. 525 per quintal from Rs. 402 per quintal. Incidently, the CIP of PDS commodities has not been revised for the last three years.

The Left parties, however, have taken a strong stand on the issue and intend to oppose tooth and nail any proposal for a major hike in the issue price at the United Front Steering Committee meeting tomorrow. Indications are that the Left parties would not mind a marginal increase in the CIP provided the hike is around Rs. 35 per quintal.

The formula was worked out at a meeting of senior finance ministry and food ministry officials here today.

Today's reporting requires specialisation in a particular subject. In the wake of liberalisation of the economy, industries are delicensed. Unlike in the past, there is no central command from where the reporter can collect all the information. Take the case of the Telecommunication Ministry, before liberalisation all the information about telecommunication could be obtained from the Telecom Minister or his secretary. Now, several multinational telecommunication companies with different technologies have tied up with the Indian companies. This requires specialisation.

Take the case of finance. Earlier, during the licence raj, if a project was approved by the government, one could get funds from banks and financial institutions at a fixed rate of interest. But now banks and FIs are under no obligations to finance projects. In the changed situation, the industrialist can either go in for GDR or raise funds from foreign banks or foreign institutional investors (FIIs).

Therefore, a financial journalist has to choose his area of specialisation even before he enters this profession. It also must be remembered that in financial journalism, it is the knowledge which is more important than the language.

In the past, people with MBA and CA shied away from financial journalism, as they thought that this job did not require specialised knowledge. The scenario has changed. Now, more and more MBA (finance) are joining financial journalism to do analytical stories and work for the investor's guide. They get a starting salary of Rs. 8,000 to Rs. 10,000 whereas reporters in the general papers get a start of Rs. 6,000 only.

Economic reporting is data-based. This information is used by the experts in the industry. This helps the industry to take decisions. A reader of an economic daily is more informed and knowledgeable than the reader of a general paper. Economic journalism has a target audience of bankers, economists and industrialists. The economic reporter should be more knowledgeable and should be cautious in writing stories.

Examples of some excellent stories done by the financial reporters:

Ambanis to withdraw from BSE

New Delhi, November 27, 1995: Enraged Ambanis have decided to delist Reliance Industries Limited (RIL) from the Bombay Stock Exchange (BSE). Angered over the BSE decision for having suspended RIL share from trading for three days last week, the company is expected to shortly send a notice to the exchange snapping the listing agreement.

This will have a major impact on BSE sensex as RIL is one of the most actively traded scrip.

Ambanis have already sought listing of its companies, including flagship RIL, on the National Stock Exchange (NSE). Simultaneous delisting from BSE, will make NSE as the leading exchange of the country. This, however, does not mean that

Reliance scrip cannot be traded on BSE. Sources said it can continue to be traded under the permitted securities list.

The delisting could mean rendering BSE sensex meaningless which may also witness a fall by about 200 points. RIL weight in 36 scrip BSE sensex was around 10 per cent on Monday.

RIL has charged BSE and its directors for having acted in a biased manner on duplicate share controversy causing grave injury to the company. They have specifically charged a few BSE directors for having conducted a sustained campaign against the company.

What angered Ambanis most was the unseeming controversy over just 40,000 duplicate shares which was equal to 0.01 per cent of RIL equity capital valued at around Rs. one crore against the total capitalisation of Rs. 10,000 crores. RIL had also asked the BSE board to investigate the role of few BSE directors who were allegedly involved in sustained bear hammering in its scrip.

While the BSE gave a clean chit to these directors, the company feels that no thorough inquiry was conducted. It is learnt that the company will soon be submitting details of speculative trading indulged into by these said directors shortly with Sebi and the Finance Ministry.

BSE had charged RIL that the company had issued 40,000 duplicate shares around the same time original share certificates had been lodged. Based on this charge, BSE ordered suspension of trading in RIL shares for a period of three days from November 16 to November 20.

This was despite the RIL's contention that originals lodged for transfer had been rejected by the transfer agency, the Reliance Consultancy Limited (RCS), as there was a signature variation for the transferor on the transfer deeds.

Reliance had also stated that the issue of duplicate shares is a normal legal process adhered to when the originals are claimed to have been lost or destroyed. There is, therefore, nothing extraordinary about this process and the company cannot be subjected to such a severe penalty such as suspension of trading in its shares.

Controversy over Concessions to MS Shoes

New Delhi: February 10, 1995: A major controversy is brewing over the Securities and Exchange Board of India (SEBI) move to allow concessions to MS Shoes on the timing of its rights issue.

According to Sebi guidelines, the gap between the closure dates of rights issue and public issue should not exceed 30 days. The public issue of MS Shoes opens on February 14 while its final closing date is not later than February 24. The rights issue will take place in April.

The catch in the whole matter is that investors applying for Rs. 700 crores public issue do not know that the presently quoted market rate of Rs. 460 is cum-rights. The stock price will become ex-rights in March and will then drop sharply to around Rs. 300 as it is a 1:1 ratio at a price of Rs. 154.

The main attraction for investing in the public issue is the price differential between the issue price and the quoted price. Market sources said the investors will see this differential vanishing in March when the rate becomes ex-rights. MS Shoes is offering zero interest convertible debentures of Rs. 199 each for cash at par in its public issue.

Merchant bankers said it is a normal practice in the corporate sector to ensure that the ex-rights price is known before the opening of the public issue. All companies either close or open the rights and public issues together. Also, all companies ensure that the public and rights issues close within 30 days, sources said.

This is perhaps the first time that any company has sought specific exemption on these grounds and has been granted by Sebi.

In its acknowledgement card to MS Shoes, Sebi has stated that the request for opening the rights issue after the conversion of pending FCDs has been acceded.

However, it is not clear on what grounds Sebi has allowed this exemption. Observers said that the least Sebi could have done was to insist on a proper disclosure in the offer document informing investors that the present market price was cum-rights and, therefore not realistic. Sebi had insisted on similar disclosures in other issues where trading volume had been thin.

According to a company spokesman, the rights issue was kept in April because the company wanted the existing debenture holders to be entitled to the rights.

Did an Aircraft Clip Russi Mody?

New Delhi: December 16, 1996: The Enforcement Directorate is investigating Mr. Russi Mody's involvement in an alleged FERA violations in the import of an aircraft by Tisco.

Aviation ministry sources say that the probe prompted the minister to ask Mr. Mody to step down from the post of chairman of the AI board.

Top officials told *The Economic Times* that Mr. Mody did not resign on his own but was forced to put in his papers.

The FERA violation case dates back to Mr. Mody's days with Tisco, where he was the executive chairman.

Confirming the investigation against Mr. Mody and two Tata group companies, finance ministry sources say that "the probe has reached a crucial stage and the final outcome may indict Mr. Mody and officials of Tata Korf and Tisco".

They say they have information indicating that Mr. Mody and other Tata officials may have indulged in dubious practices, violating Section 8 of the Fera Act.

The civil aviation ministry, realising that Mr. Mody may have to be summoned, asked him to quit, say sources in the ministry. Officials say the case pertains to the procurement of a six-seater aircraft.

The aircraft was in the possession of Tata Korf, which had acquired it as a "gift" from a London-based NRI and had registered this procurement as a "gift" in its books.

Some time later, Tata Korf handed over the aircraft to Tisco which has grounded the aircraft.

While this aircraft was a "gift", Tisco showed an expense of about $ 3 million in its accounts against the purchase of the aircraft, it is alleged.

Investigating officials suspect that on the fact of it, it appears that Tisco, under the chairmanship of Mr. Mody, had violated some sections of the Fera Act.

It is suspected that the payment for the aircraft was made by the NRI who was later reimbursed without taking a clearance from RBI.

Officials suspect if at all such a payment was made by Tisco, it would have been made through an illegal channel.

Aviation ministry sources say that ED (Enforcement Directorate) has all the information, but there is a hitch: the person who "gifted" the six-seater to Tata Korf is no more.

Chitalias drop a bomb, want to turn approver

New Delhi: September 18, 1996: A potentially ominous development for ITC, its one-time friends, Mr. Suresh Chitalia and Devang Chitalia, both US-based NRIs, have offered to turn approvers against the company.

In a letter to the Indian government, the Chitalias have said that they are prepared to spill the beans over ITCs alleged irregularities in overseas transactions worth several hundred crores, provided they are granted immunity from prosecution in India.

Finance ministry sources confirm that the offer letter has reached the Union government. It has been sent by the Chitalias' legal counsel, Mr. William Handler. The New Jersey-based lawyer has proposed in unambiguous terms that if his clients, who have sued ITC for $ 55.6 million in the US court, are not brought under the dragnet of Indian laws, they are prepared to expose the ITC's alleged *modus operandi* and how it violated RBI regulations.

It is also learnt that Chitalias have also offered to send an advance copy to the Indian government of the supplementary disposition they are planning to file in the US court.

Under Section 360 of the Indian Criminal Procedure Act, the government has the power to grant 'tender of pardon' (subject to approval by the court) to any person who vows to make complete disclosure in a particular case. Usually, the court approves the executive's decision in such cases.

In case the government takes up Chitalias' offer, things might turn out to be quite dire for top ITC executives, including its past chairman, Mr. K.L. Chugh, and its present one, Mr. Yogi Deveshwar.

As of now, the government is pondering over the offer which was made about a fortnight ago.

Sources say that ITC has got wind of the offer and some lobbying is being done through a powerful industrial group and a section of politicians. This has brought the Ministry of Finance under pressure.

Even within the finance Ministry, fissures in the bureaucracy over the issue have apparently surfaced. It is learnt that a section of the bureaucracy is in favour of granting legal immunity to Chitalias and a draft letter accepting the offer has been prepared. Sources said that 'finishing touches' were being given.

It is learnt that once immunity is granted to the Chitalias, Mr. K.L. Chugh, Mr. Y.C. Deveshwar and other top officials of the tobacco company would be questioned by the enforcement directorate.

Meanwhile, the finance ministry suspects that there is a move to settle the ITC-Chitalias' dispute out of court. Since Chitalias' disclosures may have a serious fallout on the ITC and its future relationship with BAT, a battery of professionals has been given the task to accomplish the 'mission'.

The dispute between Chitalias and the ITC cropped up over certain million-dollar outstandings. When the ITC demanded about $ 16 million from the Chitalias as damages for certain export goods, the Chitalias reacted by suing the company for $ 55.6 million.

In their disclosure affidavit before the US court, Chitalias have alleged that the ITC created overseas corporations to generate fictitious profits and bypass RBI rules.

Meanwhile, the enforcement directorate is learnt to have interrogated several second-rung executives of ITC and is likely to question the top guns soon.

Stock Market Scam—1992

The credit to expose the biggest Harshad Mehta stock market scam in the history of the country involving an amount of Rs. 3000 crores goes to Sucheta Dalal, an Assistant Business Editor, *The Times of India,* Bombay.

Sucheta Dalal is a graduate in statistics. She worked in a hotel at the initial stages and then reported in many newspapers and magazines, including the *Observer*. Her husband, Debashish Basu, is a chartered accountant and equally has a substantial work to his credit. He is the person who launched The 'Business Times' section of *The Times of India* and gave it an aggressive look.

Although they are both hotshot reporters, this was not something that they had trained for. Debashish for instance, is interested in film criticism. He got admission in the Film Institute in Pune, but chucked it up and joined *Business Today* in Bombay as an Associate Editor.

Married in March 1991, both share similar interests apart from their taste for doing challenging business stories. In music, their interests vary from Bhimsen Joshi to Perry Cuomo to Mozart. Whatever little time is available for reading is spent on professional literature. Debashish's favourite magazine being *The Economist* (London).

The nature and dimensions of the securities scam bring disturbing questions to their minds.

Both are emphatic, however, in stating that the solution to the problem does not lie in reversing the process of economic liberalisation. "What is required is more liberalisation, not less. More openness is the key. Because things were shrounded in secrecy that people like Harshad Mehta got away with dodging the system for so long", observes Sucheta.

What about the thousands of investors who lost their money in the scam? "It was their fault", says Debashish. "They are rational persons and should have weighed all the risks before investing their money."

Sucheta adds: "There are 865 million Indians and only 15 million investors in the country. Nobody should shed too many tears for their actions". (Population and investors figures are of 1991-92).

The two of them have highly self-critical attitude towards the state of business writing. Sucheta says: "People prefer to write 'positive' stuff on business houses and commercial establishments because it is less complicated and never gets rejoinders." Debashish adds: "This is because audience has been undemanding. The moment people start asking for better quality business journalism, somebody perforce have to provide it."

Both, however, do not hesitate to point out that business houses too must share the blame for the relative backwardness of business journalism in India. "Typically, most business houses do not like to share all the relevant information with the press. Often, it is very frustrating and even humiliating experience." Adds Debashish, "The securities scam has shown that the RBI, SBI and even the foreign banks have disastrous communication strategies".

Sucheta and Debashish feel that business journalists must be aggressive. But they must also be responsible. Business journalism involves people's reputation and business, unlike in other areas of journalism, everything written in business journalism has a fallout in terms of rupees.

Sucheta's story on the securities was published on the front page of *The Times of India* on April 23, 1992. The story shook the government and the country. What about the story on Harshad Mehta that catapulated her into limelight? "That was pure luck", Sucheta says.

"A person walked in to see me with an unconfirmed report of the State Bank of India activities. We made at least 50 calls. R. Srinivasan, my colleague in Delhi, who was in Bombay at that time, went to SBI, masquerading as an investor and we got around seven independent confirmations. Finally, we got a very senior SBI officer to give us the green signal. After convincing ourselves that the facts were true, we decided to run the story."

She, however, adds: "But it was very important to carry the report on the day (April 23) it appeared. The next day would have been too late as Harshad Mehta would by then have repaid Rs. 622 crores. In fact, we got approval to run the article at 10.20 at night from Dileep Padgaonkar (*The Times of India* editor). If he had gone out for a party that evening, then it would have been impossible."

Sucheta is grateful to the "consistent and unstinted support" she has received from her editor. In any other publication, the story would have been killed by vested interests".

A good business journalist knows that doing well-researched investigative story is like walking through a minefield. One must know the terrain well. As Debashish emphasises: "People tend to forget the fact that newspapers are a business too, and they are also subject to the same pulls and pressures as anyone else."

He is however a bit more cynical than Sucheta. He feels that owners of magazines and newspapers have stifled the creativity and talent of many a reporter and so far most business news has been of 'soft' nature (uncritical and eulogising articles).

But today there is a sea change in the economic reporting. Since there is competition in business reporting, a lot of hard and analytical stories are appearing in magazines and newspapers. A lot remains to be done in business reporting, but a solid beginning has been made. There is a demand for such reporting and it can no longer be suppressed. There is a shortage of experienced economic reporters who can undertake such a work.

The Securities Scam story published by *The Times of India* on April 23, 1992 ran as follows:

SBI Goof-Up in Broker Deals

By Sucheta Dalal and R. Srinivasan. Bombay, April 22 (1992): The State Bank of India (SBI) is making frantic efforts to reconcile the books of its securities and investment department in the wake of the discovery that several hundred crore rupees had been advanced without following due procedure and possibly without collateral.

According to top-level sources in the bank, the key figure is allegedly a big bull who has been in the news recently because of his huge transactions in the stock markets. A couple of other big and reputable broking houses are also said to be involved.

According to SBI sources, the respected bull operator alone, has been advanced over Rs. 500 crore. Advances to other brokers would add another couple of hundred crores to this figure.

The SBI chairman, Mr. M.N. Goiporia, denied the scam when contacted, but admitted that reconciliation was a problem. "We have very heavy transactions. SBI reconciliation is sometimes difficult," he said. Confronted specifically with the identity of the person whose transactions were under scrutiny, he said, "There is nothing that I can say."

Mr. C.L. Khemani, deputy managing director in charge of the bank's treasury and investment department, also said that reconciliations were a problem. But these would be completed in time for the audit, he added. He pointed out that SBI dealt in Rs. 10,000 crores worth of government securities and re-conciliation was difficult.

Cover-up On: However, top level sources in SBI point out that after the scandal was unearthed, 11 days ago, the bull operator was called to the bank, and has reportedly agreed to reconcile the books by paying cash and depositing securities. He is understood to have agreed to give cheques worth only Rs. eight crores and square the balance in the form of securities.

SBI sources say the scam was unearthed when an officer in the securities and investment department, who is allegedly the key figure in this operation, went on leave recently.

According to these sources, some discrepancies like cheques and delivery dates not coinciding, were discovered when a reconciliation of the department's books was done a few days ago. This triggered a major investigation by SBI authorities.

The investigation is being conducted by a team of top-level officers and the bank's vigilance department. The bank, it is believed, appears to be confident that the amount can be squared up.

Modus Operandi: The *modus operandi* appears to have been simple. The treasury department makes huge investments in the market every day. These transactions are routed through brokers. Transactions take place on the telephone and advances made against these transactions have to be backed up by the delivery of appropriate security.

Usually, temporary security is provided in the form of banker's receipts (BRs) which have to be replaced by cash or security in a couple of days. However, the officer suspected of involvement in the scam apparently failed to have the BRs converted.

This allowed the bull operator actually holding the securities to repledge them elsewhere and make a packet. The goof-up was possible because several other banks were willing to issue BRs without security.

According to SBI insiders, such operations have been on for some time, and it is surprising that it escaped detection for so long. The bankers themselves seem to have enormous faith in the suspected bull operator's ability to reconcile the books by providing the huge amount of security. (closed)

The wizard, who master-minded the scam, was flamboyant 37 year old Harshad Mehta. This was the man who would write cheques worth Rs. 500 crores to the SBI, Rs. 200 crores to the BSE to cover his stock purchases. He created a furore by paying Rs. 26 crores as advance income tax to the government, making him the biggest individual taxpayer in the country. In March 1992, he picked up Rs. 1 crore worth of ACC shares as a birthday gift to himself.

Mehta supported a fleet of foreign cars. The one most dear to him was Rs. 45 lakh Luxux car. He possessed 15,000 sq ft home in Bombay's Worli seaface area with its billiards room, mini-theatre and a nine-hole golf course.

Mehta's Operations

In 1992, banks were stifled for funds because of tight credit policy. The banks wanted to get out of this situation and make profits. And in return, they were not averse to help Harshad Mehta, even though it meant breaking rules.

Mehta's methods were not altogether new, only bigger in scope. This is what he did. SBI, like other banks wanted to buy bonds or securities issued by the government, this is essentially a debt paper issued by the government to raise money for its expenses. Banks are decreed by law to hold a certain amount securities to meet these requirements.

Securities are bought and sold routinely and daily transactions for the industry can be between Rs. 1,20,000 crores and Rs. 1,40,000 crores and are usually brokered. Mehta acted as broker for the SBI whereas he was not on the RBI's approved list of security brokers.

Mehta found securities sellers in UCO Bank and NHB, among others. These banks then issued notes—called bank receipts or BRs, acknowledging the transactions. But they did not possess the securities. It seems that by issuing receipts, the banks sold securities they did not own, a term called short-selling. They hoped that with new higher-yield bonds coming into the market, the prices of the bonds, low-yield ones, they sold initially, would go down. Then they would pick them up from the market at lower rates, making a clean profit.

Things went illegal when a covering letter instructing SBI to pay Mehta directly for the securities was sent by the seller banks. The accompanying covering letter and the bank receipt, which was made out to the SBI, were not delivered to SBI. Instead, a bank employee falsely recorded receiving them. Payments were made by SBI on the basis of these records.

This money was channelled into the stock markets. Mehta manipulated share prices by buying heavily into scrips, jacking up their prices. He then, used his inflated portfolio as collateral to raise money from banks to buy back an equal amount in government securities that was contracted for delivery to SBI, and use the seller bank—UCO or NHB—to have them delivered. The process could be rolled on endlessly, with the amount increasing each time.

Till Mehta and the banks were caught, it seemed a win-win deal for all concerned. UCO and NHB were happy with the profits that accrued to them when the prices of the bonds they had shortsold fell. SBI was happy since it did not lose anything but actual possession of a few securities from the massive Rs. 17,000 crore government securities holding. Mehta was happy with the money he got and used it to raise his stake in the stock market.

The scam got caught out when the RBI sent sleuths to check books for discrepancies, they were too many banks selling securities, they did not possess and too many banks paying for securities they did not receive.

Fall Out of the Scam

The Bombay Stock Exchange Sensitive Index crashed by 1400 points (from 4400, it came down to 3000). Small investors burnt their fingers badly. Market capitalisation fell by Rs. 1,00,000 crores. A payment crisis in the exchanges threatened to fan the spreading panic. The price of an ACC share came down to Rs. 4,750 from Rs. 9,550; Apollo Tyres to Rs. 170 from Rs. 450; Reliance Industries to Rs. 270 from Rs. 432; Mazda Industries to Rs. 150 from Rs. 1,600. These were some of the favourite shares Mehta dabbled in. About 19 banks came under scrutiny. Some of them were SBI Capital Markets, State Bank of Patiala, State Bank of Hyderabad, Standard Chartered Bank, ANZ Grindlays Bank, Citibank, Bank of America, Metropolitan Co-operative Bank, National Housing Bank, a subsidiary of RBI, the Bank of Karad, UCO Bank, Canbank Financial Services and Canara Bank Mutual Fund.

The RBI issued instructions for the liquidation of the Bank of Karad which had been exposed to this scam to the extent of Rs. 750 crores. Thousands of depositors and residents of Karad, a small town in Maharashtra accused Bhupen Dalal, a director on the board of the bank and a formidable player in the government securities market. He, later on, was arrested. It is said that Manohar J. Pherwani, Chairman of the National Housing Bank (NHB), committed suicide. NHB, is believed to be a conduit for Mehta's operations and the bank was involved to the tune of Rs. 1,200 crores in the scam.

V. Krishnamurthy, India's magic man for two decades—1972-92 was arrested and interrogated. Whatever he had touched during this period worked, from planning power projects to heading and turning around the country's biggest engineering, steel and automobile companies. He was virtually on every important committee from 1982-92. He was a member of the Planning Commission and chairman of the Committee on Public Sector Disinvestment. He enjoyed the confidence of Indira Gandhi and Rajiv Gandhi—in all a dream career.

According to investigators, the accounts of Harshad's company, Growmore Research and Asset Management, showed that a cheque for Rs. 32.74 lakhs dated March 14, 1992 had been issued in favour of K.J. Investments. The company belonged to K. Chandra and K. Jayakar, Krishnamurthy's sons. Investigators also looked into loans of Rs. 90 lakhs made by Sanwa Bank's New Delhi branch to K. J. for which Krishnamurthy had personally stood guarantee and also forex remittances made by his US-based son Jayakar.

The other angle investigating agencies looked at closely was Krishnamurthy's role in Public Sector Disinvestment Committee. He would know the money-maker and with this insider knowledge, he was in a position to manipulate sales, buying directly or through somebody else—shares cheap, and making a killing, when they are finally listed on bourses.

As chairman he was also the final decision-maker on the bids, received. In early 1992, 16 public sector units shares were grouped into 120 so-called bundles, the composition of which was not disclosed. The bids and the subsequent sale to public sector banks, fetched a total of Rs. 3,000 crores.

According to documents seized by the CBI, and from Harshad's interrogation, Krishnamurthy had discussions with him on the disinvestment issue in February 1992, though Mehta had nothing to do with it. CBI officials say Harshad advised public sector banks to bid for certain bundles. He also persuaded banks to trade shares after purchase and offered to undertake ready forward deals, buying shares at a pre-determined price.

P. Chidambaram, the Union Commerce Minister, addressed a hurriedly-convened press conference on July 9, 1992 and owned that he had a shareholding of 15,000 shares in Fairgrowth Financial Services, a Bangalore firm, under investigation in the scam. They were bought in his and his wife, Nalini's name, an advocate by profession in Madras. He offered his resignation which was accepted by Prime Minister P.V. Narasimha Rao.

On April 30, 1992, the RBI set up a committee headed by its Deputy Governor R. Janakiraman. Its brief was to examine how RBI guidelines were fluated, the culpability of those involved, the inadequacies of the system, as well as to suggest corrective measures.

The committee indicted almost all players in the market and established a clear collusion between bankers and brokers.

The following were the committee's findings:

1. Banks issued BRs for securities they did not possess.
2. Banks paid brokers for securities owned by other banks.
3. Banks issued BRs on behalf of brokers who used them to raise money.
4. The State Bank of India did 36 per cent of its transactions in securities through Harshad Mehta.
5. SBI allowed him to cash cheques made out to the SBI and other banks and got the SBI to issue cheques as per his dictates.
6. The National Housing Bank dealt in securities on behalf of other banks.
7. The general manager of the bank did not sign these deals.
8. The NHB issued BRs on behalf of other parties without any collateral or written agreements.
9. The SBI Capital Markets maintained dubious records.
10. It undertook buy-back deal in units and PSU bonds,

though prohibited from doing so under RBI guidelines.

11. The UCO Bank advanced money against promissory notes of Mehta's associates. At the repayment time, it helped Mehta by buying shares from him.
12. The Bank of Karad in order to help brokers, primarily Bhupen Dalal and Abhay D. Narottam, to raise funds, issued BRs against non-existing securities.

Ethics and Financial Reporting

Financial journalists are much in demand these days as a host of new financial newspapers and magazines have come in the market. There is also a great demand for them in the electronic media. This has opened new opportunities for students who wish to join this profession. The starting salary for journalists in this field is around Rs. 7,000. New entrants, who have begun their career as reporters, have gone up the ladder fast. For instance, in *The Economic Times* most of the reporters have become special correspondents within a period of five years drawing a salary of Rs. 15,000 to Rs. 20,000. More or less, the same is the experience of journalists in other financial dailies and magazines. The financial journalists have done equally well, if not better, on the news desk.

Some of the financial journalists, who joined *The Economic Times* during the year 1992-93 have now shifted to the electronic media with a salary of Rs. 40,000 per month, a car and other perks. Few of them have got cellular phones also.

Many students whom I taught journalism at the various colleges of the Delhi University, took to reporting after the completion of their course. But they were not satisfied with the general reporting like covering crime, courts, corporation and Delhi administration. They wanted to cover corporate news which they thought was more prestigious and soon catapulted them into influential circles. One of them rang me up after working in *The Statesman* for a year. He got eighty bylines during his short stay there. He told me that he was keen on joining financial daily and do corporate reporting. He got into *The Business Standard*, stayed there for less than a year and is now working in *The Financial Express*, Bombay, covering stock markets and doing exceedingly well.

There is so much of keenness among the journalists to join economic reporting that some of them have even offered to work on a token salary if they are taken on the staff of the paper. Recently *The Statesman* Editor Ravindran went to Calcutta to recruit some business correspondents. He was surprised to see the response. Quite a few offered to work on a token salary. It is said that a financial reporter makes about Rs. 20,000 over and above his salary every month by way of discount coupons and cash at the time of new issues. This is besides costly gifts and jaunts and rubbing shoulders with the captains of the industry.

Lately, MBAs and CAs are also joining this profession. Most of them are working for the Investor's Guide and do analytical stories on various segments of the industry and financial institutions. They provide useful information to the investors. They get a starting salary of about Rs. 8,000. Many of them have joined multinationals now at a salary of Rs. 40,000 after a short stint in *The Economic Times*.

There are plenty of temptations for financial journalists to accept gifts and jaunts. In fact, the image of the corporate reporters has been tarnished in recent times due to their succumbing to these offers. It is not without reason that many companies claim that journalists are in their pockets. There are many journalists who are on the payrolls of the companies and do public relations job for them. Sometimes, the companies insist that only a particular reporter would cover their activities. One of the editors got annoyed with the Chief Sub-Editor because he gave the name of only one of the companies in the headlines which was involved in over-invoicing. Later on, it was discovered that his wife was working in one of the outfits of this company.

Another senior journalist, who is now a consulting editor for an economic daily, run by a powerful corporate group, told me that he was being looked after by his company extremely well and that the company gave a ticket to him and his family for a jaunt in Europe. He lamented that his earlier employer where he worked for 30 years never looked after him so well.

I think there is a need for guidelines and a code for financial journalists in particular and for others in general. Journalists should resist such allurements and keep the flag of objective and independent reporting aloft. Credibility of the newspapers should not be bargained for anything.

Index